STRATEGY

A View from the Top

Cornelis A. de Kluyver

Henry Y. Hwang Dean and Professor of Management
Peter F. Drucker Graduate School of Management
Claremont Graduate University

John A. Pearce II

Endowed Chair in Strategic Management and Entrepreneurship
College of Commerce and Finance
Villanova University

Foreword by Peter F. Drucker

Prentice Hall

Prentice Hall
Upper Saddle River, NJ 07458

Library of Congress Cataloging-in-Publication Data

de Kluyver, Cornelis A.
    Strategy: a view from the top / Cornelis A. de Kluyver, John A. Pearce II; foreword by
Peter F. Drucker.
      p. cm.
    Includes bibliographical references and index.
    ISBN 0-13-008360-7
    1. Executives. 2. Leadership. 3. Management. I. Pearce, John A. II. Title.

HD38.2 .D425 2002
658.4'012–dc21

2002072428

Editor-in-Chief: Jeff Shelstad
Project Manager: Jessica Sabloff
Editorial Assistant: Kevin Glynn
Marketing Manager: Shannon Moore
Marketing Assistant: Christine Genneken
Managing Editor (Production): John Roberts
Production Editor: Renata Butera
Production Assistant: Dianne Falcone
Permissions Coordinator: Suzanne Grappi
Associate Director, Manufacturing: Vincent Scelta
Production Manager: Arnold Vila
Manufacturing Buyer: Michelle Klein
Cover Design: Kiwi Design
Composition: Progressive Information Technologies
Full-Service Project Management: Progressive Publishing Alternatives
Printer/Binder: Maple-Vail

Credits and acknowledgments borrowed from other sources and reproduced, with
permission, in this textbook appear on appropriate page within text.

Pearson Education LTD.
Pearson Education Australia PTY, Limited
Pearson Education Singapore, Pte. Ltd
Pearson Education North Asia Ltd
Pearson Education, Canada, Ltd
Pearson Educatión de Mexico, S.A. de C.V.
Pearson Education–Japan
Pearson Education Malaysia, Pte. Ltd

10 9 8 7 6 5 4 3 2 1
ISBN 0-13-008360-7

Brief Contents

Contents

List of Figures

Preface

Corporate success is increasingly tied to the ability of senior executives to craft and implement effective strategies. There is a demonstrated link between executives' strategic choices and their companies' long-term performance. The benefits accrue because companies that enjoy a substantial competitive advantage over their rivals typically have a better grasp of what their customers prefer, how they can create value, who their competitors are, and how they behave.

Formulating a sound strategy requires both analysis and synthesis, and therefore is as much a rational act as it is a creative one. Successful strategies reflect a clear strategic intent and a deep understanding of an organization's core competencies and assets. Generic strategies rarely propel a company to a leadership position. Knowing where you want to go and finding carefully considered, creative ways of getting there are the hallmarks of successful strategy.

This book is designed for practicing executives who are getting ready to assume broader responsibilities and need a short, practical, highly readable guide to strategy formulation, and for MBA and EMBA students who aspire to top management responsibilities.

ORGANIZATION

The first chapter defines strategy as the act of positioning a company for competitive advantage by focusing on unique ways to create value for customers. It contrasts strategy with operational effectiveness, links strategy development to value creation and competitive advantage, and notes the importance of organizational learning in crafting an effective strategy.

Chapter 2 looks at the importance of changes in a firm's external strategic environment—driven by economic, technological, political, and sociocultural change—and the impact of the evolutionary forces that shape an industry environment on a company's strategy formulation. In particular, we focus on two key issues that every strategist must confront: how to assess change and uncertainty and how to deal with them.

Chapter 3 focuses on the analysis of a firm's strategic resources including its physical assets, its relative financial position, the quality of its people, and specific knowledge, competencies, processes, skills, or cultural aspects of the organization.

Chapters 4 and 5 address the development of a competitive strategy at the business unit level. The principal focus of business unit or competitive strategy is on how to compete in a given competitive setting. In Chapter 4, we begin this discussion by asking: What determines profitability at the business unit level? We look at the relative importance of the nature of the industry in which a company competes, of a company's competitive position within the industry, and of the drivers that determine sustained competitive advantage. We also introduce a number of techniques that are useful for generating and assessing strategic alternatives, such as profit pool, growth vector, gap, competitor, and product life cycle analyses.

Since business unit strategy is developed in a specific industry context, Chapter 5 discusses six different industry environments. Three represent different stages in an industry's evolution—emerging, growth, and maturity. We then discuss three additional industry environments that pose unique strategic challenges—fragmented, deregulating, and hypercompetitive. Because hypercompetition is increasingly characteristic of business-level competition in many industries, we then discuss two critical attributes of successful firms in dynamic industries: speed and innovation. We conclude this chapter by considering the importance of vertical integration and horizontal thinking in business unit strategy formulation.

Chapters 6 and 7 deal with corporate strategy, which is concerned with identifying the businesses in which a company should compete and how a parent company can add value to its business units. In Chapter 6 we look at the concept of economics of scale and scope—a fundamental underpinning of corporate strategy—and try to answer the question: When is it better to be bigger? Next, we turn to the context in which corporate strategy is developed and executed. In particular, we note the importance of the dispersion in the ownership of large corporations and of the emergence of the market for corporate control. With this background, we trace the evolution of strategic thinking at the corporate level. Three perspectives are identified— the portfolio, value-based, and resource-based points of view—and their relative merits are assessed.

Chapter 7 looks at the different strategy choice options at the corporate level. We discuss concentrated growth strategies, diversification issues, merger and acquisition activities, cooperative strategies including joint ventures and alliances, and sell-offs, spin-offs, and liquidations. Next, we look at the issue of corporate management and how a parenting style affects portfolio composition. We conclude the chapter with a discussion of how to evaluate strategy choices at the corporate level.

Chapter 8 deals with formulating a global strategy. We first look at the driving forces behind the emerging global economy and characterize globalization in greater detail as an economic, political, social, and technological phenomenon. Next, we discuss industry globalization. In this section we focus on such questions as: What factors drive the globalization of industries? What explains the dominance of particular countries or regions in global industries? In the third section, we identify the principal dimensions of global strategy and introduce a framework for global strategic thinking that links global strategy options to the nature of the global industry environment. A major tenet of this discussion is that global strategy, more than strategy at the corporate or business unit levels, increasingly is played out in two arenas—a market and a nonmarket arena. We conclude this chapter with a consideration of the various strategic risk factors associated with a global strategic posture.

In Chapter 9 we identify key issues associated with implementing and controlling a chosen strategic direction. To this end, we present a conceptual framework that relates a company's strategy to its ultimate performance. This model has three primary components; the first links strategy, leadership, and corporate purpose; the second describes the organization in terms of its structure, systems, processes, people, and culture; while the third component relates performance to control.

ABOUT THE BOOK

Writing a book about a vast subject such as strategy involves making compromises and trade-offs. This book is no exception. In choosing what to include, where, and at what level of depth, we were guided by the book's primary objective—as a guide for practicing executives, MBA and EMBA students, and corporate development courses. As a consequence, we kept the book relatively short, practical, and highly readable. We adopted a broad perspective, sometimes at the expense of depth and detail about particular techniques or analysis frameworks.

We focused on the process of strategy development—not on strategic recipes. We tried to give the reader a sense of context—through the use of real examples and, where appropriate, of relevant historical references. Finally, a fundamental premise underlying this book is that strategy formulation and implementation are a dynamic process. As committed as they are to excellence in strategic decision-making, executives must remain equally committed to change. Successful implementation therefore increasingly calls for the use of change management techniques.

Acknowledgments

Writing a book is a mammoth undertaking. Fortunately, we had a lot of encouragement along the way from family members, colleagues, and friends. We take this opportunity to thank them all for their constructive criticisms, their time, and their words of encouragement. We are grateful to all of them and hope the result meets their high expectations.

We are particularly indebted to Peter F. Drucker. His endorsement of this book—in the form of a thoughtful foreword—means a lot to us. Peter's unique perspectives on the changing competitive environment have helped shape the thinking of CEOs, academics, analysts, and commentators alike. We hope this book contributes to this process.

Finally, our heartfelt thanks go to our families: Louise de Kluyver and sons Peter and Jonathan, and Susie Pearce and sons David and Mark. We thank them for their unwavering support.

Kees de Kluyver and Jack Pearce

Foreword

by

Peter F. Drucker

As Cornelis A. de Kluyver and John A. Pearce II point out in the first chapter of this book, "It is hard to imagine a business discussion that does not include the word *strategy*." Yet the term as applied to business is not even 40 years old. In Allan Nevins's 1957 definitive history of Henry Ford and the Ford Motor Company, the word *strategy* is nowhere to be found. Arguably the most successful American strategic thinker and planner, Alfred Sloan never used the term strategy in his treasure-trove book on strategic management, *My Years with General Motors.* And when I—in 1964—wanted to call my book on the subject *Business Strategies,* my publisher demurred. "Strategy," he argued, "applies to the military or to politics, but not to business." We instead called the book *Managing for Results.*

A few years later, strategy became a key concept, a buzz word, and has remained so ever since. The whiz kids who worked for Robert McNamara in the U.S. Department of Defense under Presidents Kennedy and Johnson took the term *strategy* with them as they moved out into business and academia. It immediately caught on.

There are scores of books on strategy, and new ones with *strategy* in their title. But this book, *Strategy: A View from the Top,* is to the best of my knowledge, the only one to ask: What is strategy, and why? It is the only one to ask: To what ends should strategy be managed—in and by a particular business—and how? It is the only book that is focused on managing strategy for effective action.

Specifically, this book enables executives to decide which strategic concepts and models are enduring and which are ephemeral; which contribute to business success and which have outlived their usefulness. This book enables executives to decide which specific strategies fit their business, and which apply to their own particular situation, at a given time and place, to focus on their goals and objectives.

The ability of executives to insightfully analyze their competitive arenas and to shape productive strategies is particularly important in a period of turbulence and rapid change such as the one we live in now and are likely to experience in the foreseeable future. Most businesses—large and small, purely local and multinational—are already facing new challenges to their traditional strategies. Some examples are:

- The rapidly emerging challenge to traditional organizational structures: the shift from the monolithic corporation held together by ownership, to a confederation of alliances, minority investments, partnerships, and know-how agreements held together by strategy.

- The bewildering array of ways to integrate traditional distribution and online Internet services, each of them extremely risky.
- What to outsource, when, to whom, and how.
- How to balance the functional silos, each change-resistant and parochial in its vision and values, but with a highly specialized competence, with a holistic business that knows the forest but may not know how to grow strong trees.
- The strong possibility that within the next ten years, the demographics in developing countries will split the homogeneous mass market of the late 20th century along generational lines into two or more distinct and different markets, each with its own values, habits, and distribution channels.

Every one of these challenges requires executives to make strategic decisions. And each such decision then requires something—at best barely mentioned by other books on strategy: effective action. Each challenge requires strategic management to identify the strategies that fit a particular challenge, to identify the one that is right for the specific business at this specific time, and to convert the strategy chosen into effective action. These are the subjects of *Strategy: A View from the Top*. It is an important book.

Peter F. Drucker
Claremont, California

About the Authors

Cornelis A. (Kees) de Kluyver is the Henry Y. Hwang Dean and Professor of Management at the Peter F. Drucker Graduate School of Management at the Claremont Graduate University. He is also Executive Director of the Peter F. Drucker Research Library and Archives and a Governor of the Peter F. Drucker Foundation for Non-Profit Management.

He has held prior academic appointments at George Mason University, at the University of Virginia, and at Purdue University, and for several years was a principal with Cresap Management Consultants, a Towers Perrin Company, in the firm's strategy and organizational effectiveness practice. In this position, he served a wide range of clients in the high technology and service industries on various international strategy issues including the impact of European unification on North American business and the globalization of multinational operations.

Dr. de Kluyver serves on a number of corporate, foundation, and advisory boards, is a frequent speaker to professional audiences, and holds a Ph.D. in Operations Research from Case Western Reserve, an MBA for the University of Oregon and undergraduate degrees from the University of Oregon and the Netherlands School of Business.

John A. (Jack) Pearce II holds the College of Commerce & Finance Endowed Chair in Strategic Management and Entrepreneurship at Villanova University. Twice the recipient of the Fulbright U.S. Professional Award, he received his Ph.D. degree from The Pennsylvania State University. Professor Pearce is coauthor of 32 books, and has authored more than 85 articles and 150 professional papers. The first Chairman of the Academy of Management's Entrepreneurship Division, he has received outstanding research awards from the Business Policy and Strategy, Organizational Communications, and Managerial Consultation Divisions of the Academy of Management, and from the National Association of Small Business Investment Companies, and the Association of Management Consulting Firms.

Professor Pearce has been a principal on research funded for more than $2 million by the State Council of Higher Education for Virginia, the U.S. Department of Justice, the International Association of Chiefs of Police, the U.S. Department of Commerce, the West Virginia Office of Economic and Community Development, and the U.S. Department of Transportation. A frequent leader of executive development programs and an active consultant, Professor Pearce's focus is on mission development, and strategy formulation, implementation, and control.

CHAPTER

1

What Is Strategy?

INTRODUCTION

How did Dell become the world's number one PC supplier? Will IBM's new focus on global services have staying power, or will its competitive resurgence prove temporary? What lessons can be learned from the high failure rate of dot-com companies? How important is it for a company to be first in developing a new product or entering a new market? Which elements of a strategy can be globalized? These kinds of questions lie at the heart of strategic thinking.

Understanding how a sound strategy is crafted is critical because there is a proven link between a company's strategic choices and its long-term performance. Companies that enjoy an enduring competitive advantage over their rivals typically have a better grasp of what customers want, who their competitors are, and how they can create value. Successful strategies are tailored to the needs of a particular company and market environment; generic strategies rarely propel a company to a leadership position.

Formulating an effective strategy requires *analysis* and *synthesis,* and therefore is as much an *analytic* as a *creative* process.

WHAT IS STRATEGY?

It is hard to imagine a business conversation that does not include the word *strategy.* We talk about Microsoft's Internet strategy, Coca-Cola's strategy in China, Amazon's e-business strategy, McDonald's human resource strategies, IBM's marketing strategies, Intel's technology strategy, and so on. Its frequent use would suggest that the term *strategy* is unambiguous and its meaning well understood. Unfortunately, it is not. Much of what is labeled strategy in fact has little to do with it. Numerous attempts have been made at providing a simple, descriptive definition of strategy, but its inherent complexity and subtlety preclude a one-sentence description. There is substantial agreement about its principal dimensions, however. Strategy is about *positioning* an organization for *sustainable competitive advantage.* It involves making *choices* about *which industries to participate in, what products and services to offer,* and *how to allocate corporate resources.* Its primary goal is to *create value for shareholders and other stakeholders* by providing *customer value.*

Strategy Versus Tactics

New business concepts, technologies, and ideas are born every day. The Internet, innovation, total quality, flexibility, and speed, for example, all have come to be recognized as essential to a company's competitive strength and agility. As a result, corporations continue to embrace initiatives such as quality management, time-based competition, benchmarking, outsourcing, partnering, reengineering, and a host of other concepts in an all-out effort to enhance competitiveness.

Some of these initiatives have produced dramatic results. General Motors and Ford each have spent billions of dollars reengineering their design and production processes. As a result, unit costs have fallen dramatically, quality has gone up, relationships with component manufacturers and other suppliers are stronger, and the time needed to take a new car from concept to production has been cut in half. Though such results are gratifying, it is important to put them in their proper context. Enhancing operational effectiveness is crucial in today's cutthroat competitive environment, but it is no substitute for sound strategic thinking. There is a critical difference between strategy and the application of operational tools and managerial philosophies focused on operational effectiveness. Both are essential to competitiveness. But whereas the application of managerial tools is aimed at doing things better than competitors and therefore tactical in nature, strategy focuses on doing things differently. Understanding this distinction is critical, as recent history has shown. Companies that embraced the Internet as the strategic answer to their business rather than just another, if important, new tool were in for a rude awakening. By focusing too much on e-business options at the expense of broader strategic concerns, many found themselves chasing customers indiscriminately, trading quality and service for price, and with it, losing their competitive advantage and profitability.

Long-term, sustainable superior performance—the ultimate goal of strategy—can only be realized if a company can *preserve* meaningful differences between itself and its rivals. E-business initiatives, total quality management, time-based competition, benchmarking, and other tactics aimed at improved operational performance, however desirable and necessary, are generally fairly easily imitated. Enhanced performance attributable to such actions is at best temporary.

Strategy Forces Trade-offs

Strategic thinking, instead, focuses on taking *different* approaches to delivering customer value, on choosing *different* sets of activities that cannot easily be imitated, and thereby providing a basis for an enduring competitive advantage. When Dell Computer pioneered its highly successful direct sales, made-to-order business model, it carefully designed every aspect of its manufacturing, sourcing, and inventory system to support its low-cost, direct sales strategy. In the process, it redefined value for many customers in terms of speed and cost, and created major barriers to imitation. Its competitors, stuck with traditional distribution networks and manufacturing models, faced a difficult choice: abandon their traditional business model or focus on alternative ways of delivering customer value.

Thus, whereas operational effectiveness tools can improve competitiveness they do not—by themselves—force companies to choose between entirely different, internally consistent *sets* of activities. IBM and other competitors could have responded to Dell's innovative strategy by also selling directly to end users, but they would have had to dismantle their traditional distribution structures to reap the benefits Dell realizes from its strategy. Thus, choosing a *unique competitive positioning*—the essence of strategy—forces trade-offs in terms of what to do, and equally important, of what *not* to do, and creates *barriers to imitation*.

Focusing on Value Creation

Strategy should focus on creating *value*—for shareholders, partners, suppliers, employees, and the community—by satisfying the needs and wants of customers better than anyone else. If a company can deliver value to its customers better than its rivals can over a sustained period of time, that company likely has a superior strategy. This is not a simple task. Customers' wants, needs, and preferences change, often rapidly, as they become more knowledgeable about a product or service, as new competitors enter the market, and as new entrants redefine what value means. As a result, what is valuable today might not be valuable tomorrow. The moral of this story is simple but powerful: *The value of a particular product or service offering, unless constantly maintained, nourished, and improved, erodes with time.*

Figure 1-1 depicts this competitive advantage cycle. It shows that, at any given point in time, companies compete with a particular mix of resources. Some of the assets and capabilities are better than those of their rivals; others are inferior. The superior assets and capabilities are the source for positional advantages.[1] Whatever competitive advantage a firm possesses, it must expect that ongoing change in the strategic environment and competitive moves by rival firms continuously work to erode it. Competitive strategy thus has a dual purpose: slowing the erosion process by protecting current sources of advantage against the actions of competitors, and investing in new capabilities that form the basis for the next position of competitive advantage. The creation and maintenance of advantage are therefore a continuous process.

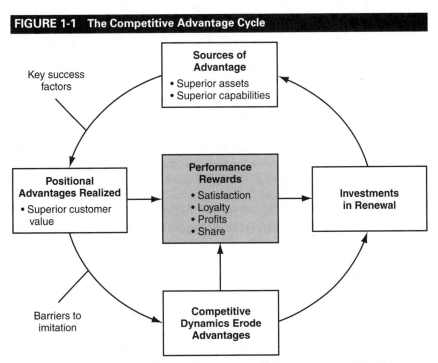

FIGURE 1-1   The Competitive Advantage Cycle

Source: WHARTON on Dynamic Competitive Strategy by George S. Day and David J. Reibstein. Copyright © 1997 by John Wiley & Sons, Inc. This material is used by permission of John Wiley & Sons, Inc.

Allowing for Learning and Adaptation

When we characterize strategy formulation as crafting a blueprint for an organization's future this should not be interpreted as deciding on a detailed long-term plan and following it to the letter. Rapid change in the competitive environment makes such a view of strategy untenable. At the time a strategy is crafted, some elements of that strategy are more predictable than others. When Intel invests in a new technology, for example, it might know that this technology holds promise in several markets. Its precise returns in different applications, however, might not be known with any degree of certainty until much later.[2] Formulating strategy therefore is about crafting a long-term *vision* for an organization, but maintaining a degree of flexibility about how to get there and preserving options for adapting to change. *Learning* is an essential component of strategy development. As soon as a company begins to implement a chosen direction, it starts to learn—about how well attuned the chosen direction is to the competitive environment, about how rivals are likely to respond, and about how well prepared the organization is to carry out its mission. Creating and preserving options for adapting to change—in the competitive or regulatory environment—therefore are key to effective strategy formulation.

A Long-Term Perspective

A long-term perspective is critical to strategic success. Oracle Corporation provides a good example. For more than a decade, the number two software maker grew at a modest pace while the PC industry exploded and Microsoft became the dominant player. Oracle, after its initial success as a Silicon Valley start-up, seemed to focus on the wrong segments. The company's database software, with its ability to organize masses of information, was an important but unexciting component of corporate computing.

Oracle, however, steadfastly focused on the long run. Envisioning a day when companies would shift many of their internal operations to the Internet, the company focused on developing software that would allow an expansion of Web-based database management capabilities to a host of other corporate tasks such as purchasing and managing inventory. The company's patience and persistence are paying off. A growing number of customers such as Ford, Chevron, and Sears use Oracle software to make large amounts of information—from product catalogs to supply contracts and order books to service manuals—instantly available to customers and employees.

Oracle's success has prompted its rivals to reexamine their strategies. Microsoft, in collaboration with SAP and others, is mounting a strong counterattack, and IBM has unleashed its consulting and sales team to sell Siebel's customer-management software, foreshadowing a further increase in rivalry.[3]

The Role of Stakeholders

Responding to the concerns and influence of the full range of an organization's *stakeholders* is also an important element of effective strategy formulation. Historically, the attention paid to stakeholders other than directly affected parties such as employees or major investors in crafting strategy has been limited. As executives learned that continuous development of internal and external resources is increasingly important to an organization's success, however, *stakeholder analysis*—the process of identifying and prioritizing key stakeholders, assessing their needs and concerns, and incorporating their ideas and insights into the strategy formulation process—has become an important element of strategy development.

Many companies rely, to a great extent, on a network of external stakeholders—suppliers, partners, and even competitors—in creating value for customers. The motivation of internal stakeholders—directors, top executives, middle managers, and employees—is also critical to success. A misstep in managing suppliers, a major error in employee relations, or a lack of communication with principal shareholders can set back a company's progress for years. The importance of different stakeholders to a company's competitive position depends on the *stake* they have in the organization and the kind of *influence* they can exert. Stakeholders can have an *ownership stake* (shareholders, directors, among others), an *economic stake* (creditors, employees, customers, suppliers, etc.), or a *social stake* (regulatory agencies, charities, the local community, activist groups, etc.).[4] Some have *formal power,* others *economic* or *political power.* Formal power is usually associated with legal obligations or rights. Economic power is derived from an ability to withhold products, services, or capital, whereas political power is rooted in an ability to persuade other stakeholders to influence the behavior of an organization.

Levels of Strategy

Strategy formulation occurs at the *corporate* and *business unit* levels. In a single product or service business, *business unit* strategy is concerned with deciding what product or service to offer, how to manufacture or create it, and how to take it to the marketplace. In a multibusiness, diversified corporation, *corporate* strategy defines a second set of issues concerning what kinds of businesses a firm should compete in, and how the overall portfolio of businesses should be managed. The strategic activities at both levels constitute *strategic management*—the totality of managerial processes used to chart and direct the future of a corporation.

THE CHANGING STRATEGY CONTEXT

Boundaries between public and private, and foreign and domestic corporations; among producers, intermediaries, partners, suppliers, and customers; and, as a consequence, between strategic partners and rivals are increasingly blurring. Many companies simultaneously compete in some segments or product lines and cooperate, through alliances, joint ventures, or supply arrangements in others. This growing complexity of the competitive landscape and the blurring of strategic roles have created new strategic challenges. Companies must uncover, analyze, and evaluate a substantially wider array of strategy options than ever before—on a global scale, and at greater speed—and be prepared to venture into often unfamiliar economic, political, technological, and cultural environments. They also must be willing to discard strategies and business models that no longer work, and quickly adopt bold, new, and often risky strategies. In doing so, they must embed continuous learning and innovation into their corporate cultures to implement them, and exercise strategic discipline to retain focus and stakeholder endorsement.

Manufacturing companies such as Intel and Motorola are questioning, for example, how much they should focus on building physical assets to create long-term competitive advantage at a time when competition is increasingly driven by knowledge and ideas, and forging key strategic alliances might be more conducive to success. They are also reevaluating what form such investments should take as mass production and consumption concepts are being displaced in some markets by a focus on tailoring products and services to the individual tastes and preferences of consumers and partners.

In this changing environment, other strategic maxims are coming under greater scrutiny. Conventional wisdom holds, for example, that (1) market share is the most appropriate measure of market influence, (2) relative share is a proxy for competitive strength, and (3) market share is a principal driver of profitability. As outsourcing becomes a more important element of strategy, however, we must distinguish between a company's market share and manufacturing or service-delivery share. Increasingly, companies compete with branded as well as nonbranded product entries, often bundled with a growing set of services, and with alliance partners rather than on their own. In this context, we should ask what market share means and how it can usefully be measured.

FORMULATING STRATEGY

Process

In crafting a strategy, it is useful to organize the process around three key questions: *Where are we now? Where do we go?* and *How do we get there?* (Figure 1-2). Each question defines a part of the process and suggests different types of analyses and evaluations. It also shows that the components of a strategic analysis overlap, and that feedback loops are an integral part of the process.

1. The *Where are we now?* part of the process is concerned with assessing the current state of the business or the company as a whole. It begins with revisiting such fundamental issues as: What is the organization's mission? What is management's long-term vision for the company? and Who are its principal stakeholders? Other key components include a detailed evaluation of the company's current performance, an assessment of pertinent trends in the broader sociopolitical, economic, legal, and technological environment in which the company operates, of opportunities and threats in the industry environment, and of internal strengths and weaknesses.

2. *Where do we go?* questions are designed to generate and explore strategic alternatives based on the answers obtained to the first question. At the business unit level, for example, options such as concentrating on growth in a few market segments or adopting a wider market focus, whether to go it alone or partner with another company, or whether to focus on value-added or low-cost solutions for customers might be considered. At the corporate level, this part of the process is focused on shaping the portfolio of businesses the company participates in, and on making adjustments in parenting philosophies and processes. At both levels, the output is a statement of *strategic intent,* which identifies the guiding business concept or driving force that will propel the company forward.

3. The *How do we get there?* component is focused on how to achieve the desired objectives. One of the most important issues addressed at this stage is how to bridge the *capability gap* that separates current organizational skills and capabilities from those needed to achieve the stated strategic intent. It deals with the strategic alignment of *core competences* with *emerging market needs,* and with identifying *key success factors* associated

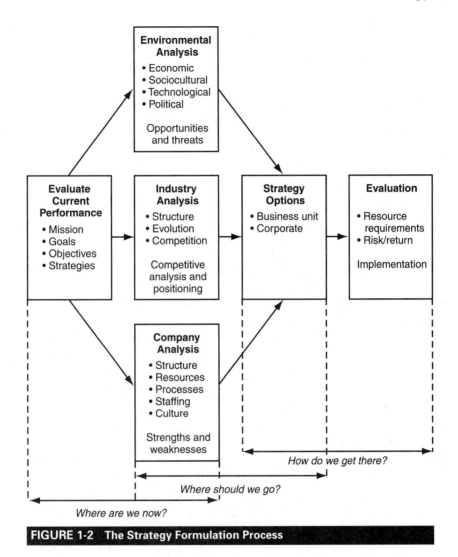

FIGURE 1-2   The Strategy Formulation Process

with successfully implementing the chosen strategy. The end product is a detailed set of initiatives for implementing the chosen strategy and exercising strategic discipline and control.

Mission and Vision

Most companies have a *mission* statement that documents the purpose for their existence, and often contains a code of corporate conduct to guide management in implementing the mission. A *vision* statement is different; it represents senior management's long-range goals—a description of what competitive position the company wants to attain over a given period of time, and what core competencies it must acquire to get there. As such, it summarizes a company's broad strategic focus for the future.

The usefulness of a carefully crafted mission statement is illustrated by the history of Johnson & Johnson. For more than 50 years, its credo—a statement of fundamental beliefs about how the company defines its corporate responsibilities—has guided Johnson & Johnson in all its actions. It begins "We believe our first responsibility is to the doctors, nurses, and patients, to mothers and fathers and all others who use our products and services" and continues to explicitly define the company's responsibilities to employees, the community, and shareholders. Its value was reaffirmed during the Tylenol crises of 1982 and 1986 when the company's product was adulterated with cyanide. With Johnson & Johnson's name and reputation at stake, executives made important decisions that were inspired by the company's credo. It helped the company preserve its reputation and regain its Tylenol acetaminophen business.

In crafting a vision statement, there are two important lessons worth heeding. First, few organizations have achieved greatness by being all things to all consumers. Focusing on relatively few activities and doing them extremely well is the hallmark of most successful companies. McDonald's became successful precisely because it stuck to hamburgers, H&R Block because it concentrates on tax preparation, and Dell Computer because it focuses on PCs. This suggests that effective strategy development is as much about deciding what not to do as it is about choosing what activities to focus on. The second lesson is that most successful companies achieved their leadership position by adopting a vision far greater than their resource base and competencies would allow. To get to a position of market leadership, a focus on the drivers of competition is not enough; strong leadership aimed at creating a new future is required. With such a mindset, disparities between resources and goals become challenges rather than constraints, and winning becomes a corporate obsession that is capable of sustaining a sense of urgency for a long period of time.[5]

A good vision provides both strategic guidance and motivational focus. An effective vision statement meets three criteria: (1) It must be clear but not so constraining that it inhibits initiative. (2) It should be desirable in the sense that it meets the legitimate interests and values of all stakeholders. (3) It must be feasible, that is, it must be implementable.[6]

Vision statements help frame strategic action. When Jack Welch became CEO of General Electric in 1981, the U.S. economy was in recession. High interest rates and a strong dollar exacerbated the problem. To get the company moving and leverage performance in GE's diverse portfolio of businesses, the new CEO challenged each business to be "better than the best." This challenge led to the adoption of the vision statement that each business become "the #1 or #2 competitor in its industry—or to disengage."

Strategic Intent and Stretch

Mission and vision statements are mostly inputs to the strategy development process; they guide the criteria by which a strategy is crafted, and define the range of options a company will consider. In contrast, a statement of *strategic intent* is both an input to and an output of the process. It is at once an executive summary of the strategic goals a company has adopted and a motivational message. Strategic intent does more than paint a vision for the future; it signals the desire to win, and recognizes that successful strategies are built as much around what can be as around what is. It focuses the organization on key competitive targets, and provides goals about which competencies to develop, what kinds of resources to harness, and what segments to concentrate on. Instead of worrying about the degree of fit between current resources and opportunities, it shifts the focus to how to close the capability gap. Current resources and capabilities become starting points for strategy development, not constraints on strategy formulation or its implementation.[7]

A related idea is the concept of *stretch.* Stretch reflects the recognition that successful strategies are built as much around *what can be* as around *what is.* Ultimately, every company must create a fit between its resources and its opportunities. The question is over what time frame? Too short a time frame encourages a focus on *fit* rather than *stretch,* on resource *allocation* rather than getting more value from existing resources. The use of too long a time horizon, on the other hand, creates an unacceptable degree of uncertainty and threatens to turn stretch objectives into unrealistic goals.

Strategy and Planning

A strategy review can be triggered by a host of factors—new leadership, disappointing performance, changes in ownership, the emergence of new competitors or technologies—or be part of a scheduled, typically annual, review process.

Thirty years ago, the term *strategic planning* was used to refer to strategy formulation. Elaborate planning processes, supported by dedicated staff groups, could be found in almost every Fortune 500 company. The process provided focus to strategy development. Then a backlash developed and strategic planning quickly fell out of favor. Disappointing corporate results, an erosion in competitiveness, a lack of innovation, and a failure to take risk all were blamed on strategic planning. An overreliance on simplistic planning models and the dubious numbers they generated was also cited as a major cause of failure. In response, formal, bureaucratic processes were replaced by simpler, more effective ones; elaborate planning systems gave way to leaner, more decentralized forms of strategy development; and staff groups that had been the backbone of many corporate planning processes were eliminated. Strategy formulation became a line management function once again; and processes that were exclusively top-down in nature were replaced by approaches that involved managers at all levels, reflecting the new culture of empowerment. In the process, thick strategic planning documents were exchanged for more easily grasped and communicated five-page strategic plans.

Although the sentiments behind these changes—making strategy development a line responsibility once again, restoring the balance between top-down and bottom-up influences, and simplifying planning processes—were laudable, their implementation often left a lot to be desired. As a result, for many companies these changes exacted a heavy price. In the frenzy of catching up with their competitors, executives became preoccupied with tactics and operational issues such as reengineering, benchmarking, downsizing, total quality initiatives, teamwork, and empowerment. Execution and implementation became the focal points of managerial effort. Strategy was easy, thought some, who believed that implementation was the real challenge.

Reaching a position of long-term, sustained superior performance requires both *strategic thinking* and *strategic planning.* Strategic thinking is focused on creating a vision for the future of the organization, and crafting a clear, concise blueprint for realizing that vision. Strategic planning is a process used to develop supporting analyses, and to communicate and implement the chosen strategy. Only a CEO or senior management can drive the strategic thinking process. Strategic thinking starts at the top of the organization, and is essentially an iterative process that through a series of exchanges works its way down to involve every level of the organization.

Strategic planning techniques and practices are once again getting more attention, albeit in much more modest proportions. General Electric, for example, once thought of as the paragon of old-style strategic planning, is pioneering new planning concepts aimed at making sure that strategic lessons learned in one part of the corporation or the globe are readily available to others. The focus of many of these new concepts and techniques is on maintaining a strategic focus and discipline, effective communication, and the rapid transfer of usable knowledge from one part of the company to another, reflecting strategic planning's new supporting role in formulating business unit and corporate strategies.

EVALUATING STRATEGIC OPTIONS

Criteria

The ultimate test of any strategy is whether it produces a sustainable competitive advantage with above-average returns. Thus, it is not surprising that to many executives strategy evaluation is principally a matter of how well a business or company performs. Although intuitive, this perspective is not satisfactory because measures of current performance are not necessarily indicative of future performance. Strategy evaluation should focus on a firm's future competitiveness and ask whether long-term objectives are appropriate; whether strategies chosen to attain such objectives are consistent, bold enough, and achievable; and whether these strategies are likely to produce a sustainable competitive advantage with above-average returns.

Quantifying such judgments is difficult. Though financial returns are important, the key issue is whether strategic intent and specific proposals aimed at realizing intent always can be reduced to a cash-flow forecast. Clearly, the financial effect on the corporation of specific strategy options, such as acquisitions at the corporate level or specific new product or market entries at the business unit level, can and should be quantified. A good argument can be made, however, that strategic thinking does not lend itself to purely quantitative assessments. Historically, corporate and business unit strategies were limited to market-based, competitive initiatives. Today, analysis of political and other nonmarket forces is becoming a more important component of strategic thinking.

Executives face enormous pressure from within the organization and from external sources such as the financial community to forecast business unit and corporate performance and, implicitly, to quantify anticipated strategic outcomes. Traditionally, *return on investment* (ROI) was the most common measure for evaluating a strategy's efficacy. Today, *shareholder value* is one of the most widely accepted yardsticks.

Shareholder Value

The *shareholder value approach* (SVA) to strategy evaluation holds that the value of the corporation is determined by the discounted future cash flows it is likely to generate. In economic terms, value is created when companies invest capital at returns that exceed the cost of that capital. Under this model, new strategic initiatives therefore are treated as any other investment the company makes, and evaluated on the basis of shareholder value. A whole new managerial framework—*value-based management* (VBM)—has been created around it.[8]

The use of shareholder value or related measures such as *economic value added* (EVA), defined as after-tax operating profit minus the cost of capital, as the principal yardstick for evaluating alternative strategy proposals is somewhat contentious. Besides implementation problems, there are issues of transparency in the relationship between shareholder value on the one hand and positioning for sustained competitive advantage on the other. Even though shareholder value and strategy formulation are ultimately about the same thing—generating long-term sustained value—they use different conceptions of value and view the purpose of strategy from a fundamentally different point of view.

Strategists focus on creating a sustainable competitive advantage through *value delivered to customers*. But SVA measures *value to shareholders*. Though in the long run the two should be highly correlated, individual strategy proposals may force short-term trade-offs between the two. It is not surprising, therefore, that shareholder value has not been universally embraced as the preferred method for measuring a strategy's potential. It also explains why less restrictive, but possibly less rigorous evaluation schemes, such as the Balanced Scorecard, discussed in Chapter 3, have gained in acceptance in the last few years.[9]

THE EVOLUTION OF STRATEGIC THINKING

The evolution of strategic thinking reflects a gradual shift in focus from an *industrial economics* to a *resource-based* to a *human and intellectual* capital perspective (Figure 1-3). It is important to understand the reasons underlying this evolution because they reflect a changing view of what strategy is, and how it is crafted.

The earlier *industrial economics* perspective held that environmental influences—particularly those that shape industry structure—were the primary determinants of a company's success. The competitive environment was thought to impose pressures and constraints, which made certain strategies more attractive than others. Carefully choosing where to compete—selecting the most attractive industries or industry segments—and controlling strategically important resources therefore became the dominant themes of strategy development, at both the business unit and corporate levels. The focus, therefore, was on *capturing economic value* through adept positioning; and industry analysis, competitor analysis, segmentation, positioning, and strategic planning became the most important tools for analyzing strategic opportunity.[10]

As globalization, the technology revolution, and other major environmental forces picked up speed and began to radically change the competitive landscape, key assumptions underlying the industrial economics model came under scrutiny. Should the competitive environment be treated as a constraint on strategy formulation or was strategy really about shaping competitive conditions? Was the assumption that businesses should control most of the relevant strategic resources needed to compete still applicable? Were strategic resources really as mobile as the traditional model assumed, and was the advantage associated with owning particular resources and competencies therefore necessarily short-lived?

Competitive Focus	Products and Markets	Resources and Competencies	Talents and Dreams
Strategic objective	Defensible product-market positions	Sustainable advantage	Continuous self-renewal
Tools/perspectives	• Industry analysis; competitor analysis • Segmentation and positioning • Strategic planning	• Core competencies • Resource-based strategy • Networks	• Vision/values • Flexibility and innovation • Entrepreneurship
Key strategic resource	Financial capital	Organizational capability	Human and intellectual capital

FIGURE 1-3   The Evolving Focus of Strategy

Reprinted from "Building Competitive Advantage Through People," by Christopher A. Bartlett and Sumantra Ghoshal, *MIT Sloan Management Review*, Winter 2002, pp. 34–41, by permission of publisher. Copyright © 2002 by Massachusetts Institute of Technology. All rights reserved.

In response to these questions, strategists have urged a shift from the industrial economics to a *resource-based* view of strategic thinking. Instead of focusing on positioning a company within environment-dictated constraints, they proposed that strategic thinking should focus on building core capabilities that transcend the boundaries of traditional business units; on creating corporate portfolios around *core businesses,* and on adopting goals and processes aimed at enhancing *core competencies.*[11] This new paradigm reflected a shift in focus from capturing economic value to *creating* value through the development and nurturing of key resources and capabilities. Instead of focusing on exploiting potential synergies between component businesses to create a competitive advantage, it stresses the importance of a fit between existing and to-be-developed corporate resources and product markets.[12]

The current focus on *human and intellectual capital* as a company's key strategic resource is a natural extension of the resource-based view of strategy. For a majority of companies, access to physical or financial resources no longer is an impediment to growth or opportunity; not having the right people or knowledge has become the limiting factor. Microsoft scans the entire pool of U.S. computer science graduates every year to identify and attract the few it accepts. It recognizes that competency-based strategies are dependent on people, that scarce knowledge and expertise drive product development, and that personal relationships with clients are key to market responsiveness.[13]

MAJOR ISSUES IN STRATEGIC MANAGEMENT

The major issues in strategic management analysis are captured by the five Cs of strategy: *content, context, conduct, change, and control. Content* refers to what strategy formulation is all about—its scope, focus, and major dimensions. *Context* refers to the setting in which a strategy is formulated. Strategy is not formulated in a vacuum; its development should be responsive to the needs and concerns of an organization's stakeholders, the strategic environment in which it operates, and a realistic appraisal of what can be accomplished. *Conduct* refers to process. Not all organizations deal with strategy formulation in the same way. In entrepreneurial organizations the process is often less formal than in large corporations; it is different in nonprofit organizations than in for-profit enterprises. Strategy formulation often reflects leadership style. Fourth, today, more than ever before, strategy must deal with continuous, sometimes abrupt *change,* in the broader economic, technological, political, and sociocultural environment, as well as in the increasingly global competitive environment. Anticipating and capitalizing on change have therefore become key determinants of success. Finally, strategic discipline and *control* will prove increasingly important in the years ahead as the number of available strategy options multiplies and windows of opportunity to capitalize on them become shorter.

NOTES

1. George S. Day, "Maintaining the Competitive Edge: Creating and Sustaining Advantages in Dynamic Competitive Environments," Chapter 2, p. 52, in George S. Day and David J. Reibstein (eds.), *Wharton on Dynamic Competitive Advantage* (New York: John Wiley & Sons, 1997).

2. These ideas are based on Timothy A. Luehrman, "Strategy as a Portfolio of Real Options," *Harvard Business Review* (Sept.– Oct. 1998), pp. 89–99.

3. "Oracle, Why It's Cool Again," *Business Week Online,* May 8, 2000.

4. R. E. Freeman, *Strategic Management: A Stakeholder Approach* (Boston: Pittman, 1984).

5. Gary Hamel and C. K. Prahalad, "Strategic Intent," *Harvard Business Review* (May–June 1989), pp. 63–76.

6. John Kotter, *A Force for Change* (New York: Free Press, 1990).

7. Hamel and Prahalad, "Strategic Intent."

8. See for example Tom Copeland, Tim Koller, and Jack Murrin, *Valuation: Measuring and Managing the Value of Companies* (McKinsey & Company, New York: Wiley & Sons, 1995).

9. R. S. Kaplan and D. P. Norton, "Using the Balanced Scorecard as a Strategic Management System," *Harvard Business Review* (Jan.–Feb. 1996), pp. 75–85; and R. S. Kaplan and D. P. Norton, "The Balanced Scorecard—Measures That Drive Performance," *Harvard Business Review* (Jan.–Feb. 1992), pp. 71–79.

10. Christopher A. Bartlett and Sumantra Ghoshal, "Building Competitive Advantage Through People," *Sloan Management Review,* 2002, 43, 2, pp. 34–41.

11. C. K. Prahalad and G. Hamel, "The Core Competence of the Corporation," *Harvard Business Review* (May–June 1990), pp. 79–91.

12. David J. Collis and Cynthia A. Montgomery, *Corporate Strategy: Resources and Scope of the Firm,* Chicago: Irwin, 1997, p. 17.

13. Bartlett and Ghoshal, "Building Competitive Advantage Through People," p. 35.

CHAPTER

Change and Uncertainty in the External Strategic Environment

INTRODUCTION

An effective strategy anticipates and capitalizes on relevant changes in a company's strategic environment. This chapter has three parts. First, we consider the influence of changes in a firm's *external strategic environment*—driven by *economic, technological, political,* and *sociocultural* changes—on the evolving competitive environment and strategy formulation. Next, we look at the evolutionary forces that shape a company's *industry environment.* Finally, we present an analytic framework for analyzing *change* and *uncertainty* and assessing their effects on strategic choice. Chapter 3 will consider the effect of a firm's *internal company environment* on strategy formulation.

Changes in the broader *economic, technological, political,* and *sociocultural environment,* often beyond the control of any single company, can have a profound effect on success. Demographic or social changes, such as the aging of the population, the entry of large numbers of women into the labor force, or the renewed interest in quality-of-life issues can create new opportunities or threaten existing businesses. The technology revolution has changed the way we live, work, and unwind, and spawned a number of new industries. Globalization has increased the interdependence between the world's major economies and intensified competition in many industries.

Changes in a company's *industry environment* typically have a more direct and pronounced effect on a company's strategic options than changes in the broader strategic environment. Consider the enormous changes taking place in the telecommunications industry. Deregulation has transformed an industry that consisted of a number of well-defined regulated services into a fully integrated information services industry. Telecommunications companies are making inroads into mail and overnight delivery of information, the Internet is progressively supplanting voice communications, cable TV has entered the two-way communications race, and broadcast TV and satellite-based communications are going digital.

Some changes, such as demographic shifts, are predictable. Others, like an oil crisis or a terrorist attack, take us by surprise. Scanning the environment for forces that potentially have a major influence on a company's fortunes can lessen uncertainty and therefore is an important component of strategic analysis. Most companies routinely follow economic trends such as the growth of a country's gross domestic product (GDP), interest rates, inflation, and employment. Monitoring new technological developments has also become an integral part of many companies' strategy development process. Trends in the legal/political arena or in sociocultural aspects of our environment are typically followed on a less formal basis but are assuming greater importance in many industries.

CHANGE IN THE EXTERNAL ENVIRONMENT

In *Management Challenges for the 21st Century,* Peter Drucker discusses five transforming forces that can be considered certainties: (1) demographic change—the collapsing birthrate in the developed world, (2) shifts in the distribution of disposable income and the emergence of new growth industries, (3) the quest for defining and delivering performance, (4) the need for global competitiveness for all institutions, and (5) the growing incongruence between economic globalization and political splintering.[1] Each of these trends is likely to have major implications for the long-term strategies of companies, not-for-profit organizations, and governments around the world.

Demographic Change—The Collapsing Birthrate in the Developed World

Of all the social changes in the Western world—from the increased participation of women in the work force and the postponement of marriage, more divorces, and smaller families to the emergence of ethnic consumer groups and the proliferation of more varied lifestyles—none will have as great an influence as the gradual aging of the population.

The average age of the U.S. population is expected to increase from nearly 28 in 1970 to almost 40 by the middle of this century. This phenomenon is not limited to the United States; European countries and Japan are experiencing a similar trend. The massive increase in the number of senior citizens—the result of lower birthrates, advances in healthcare, and a host of other societal factors—creates enormous opportunities for companies attuned to this trend. For others, it can be threatening. Demand for specialized products and services targeted at senior citizens—from assisted living to healthcare to new forms of transportation to a whole array of specialized financial services—will grow substantially in the years to come. At the same time, those counting on a continuation of a strong youth culture may be in for a rude awakening.

The Distribution of Disposable Income and New Growth Industries

Advances in technology continue to fuel a major shift from an economy focused on producing physical goods to one powered by knowledge and ideas. This giant economic shift from goods to ideas explains the emergence of entirely new growth industries—from financial and information services to assisted living to biotechnology. It also has changed the very *nature* of strategic opportunity and risk. In an Internet-based economy, ideas spread across the world almost overnight at an extremely low cost. This has created opportunities for enormous returns for entrepreneurs with the right idea at the right time. The potential for above average, relatively quick returns, in turn, has encouraged the formation of vast pools of venture capital and pushed up valuations to often-unsustainable levels. In this fast-paced competitive environment, distinguishing scarce good ideas from amply available bad ideas has therefore become even more of a challenge.

The Quest for Defining and Delivering Performance

Global competition has substantially increased choices for consumers, producers, and shareholders. Consumers have more choice over where and how they spend their money, producers have more choice over which suppliers or distribution alternatives to use, and shareholders have more choice over where to invest. At the same time, advances in technology have created more opportunities for individuals and firms to collect information and conduct economic activity outside traditional structures.

This growth in choice and in access to information about choices, and the resultant increase in competition, is reshaping the drivers of competition. Large and small companies alike are finding that being lean and flexible, and having a strong reputation (brand) and highly talented people, among other factors, have become more important than ever to success. General Electric is huge, but also lean. Like GE, firms will continue to flatten their management structures as improvements in communication technology increase the number of employees that supervisors can manage effectively.

One way companies are trying to become more flexible is through outsourcing and partnering—lifetime employment is almost a phenomenon of the past. With enduring competitive advantages becoming scarcer and harder to realize, companies are looking more to branding and the use of images that can cut through the clutter of choices. Increasingly, the real economic value of a corporation does not come from the assets it owns but from the domain of trust that it establishes with its customers. A key challenge, therefore, is to maintain the quality of a brand while at the same time subcontracting a substantial portion of the value-creation process to other companies. Finally, the human side of management is set to become more—rather than less—important. Increasingly, what sets companies apart is their ability to create and innovate. Hiring, motivating, and retaining the best people have become of paramount concern.

The new competitive environment has also exposed differences in how performance is defined and measured in various regions of the world. The emergence of a global market for equity has put pressure on companies to align performance metrics and provide greater transparency and accountability to shareholders. The last century saw a range of challenges to shareholder capitalism: from state-owned capitalism, from mixed stakeholder capitalism as practiced in many European economies, from the managerial capitalism of 1950s America, from the Japanese and Korean stakeholder philosophies, and even, to some extent, from the virtual economy of the Internet. Long-term shareholder value creation has become the principal corporate performance objective globally. It is interesting to note, for example, that Germany has introduced more initial public offerings (IPOs) in the last 5 years than in the previous 50 years combined, and the number of shareholders there has surpassed the number of trade unionists.

The Need for Companies to Be Globally Competitive

Boundaries between countries and regions may have meaning in political terms but have all but disappeared on the global competitive map. The ever-faster flow of information across the world has made people aware of the tastes, preferences, and lifestyles of citizens in other countries. Through this information flow we are all becoming—at varying speeds and at least in economic terms—global citizens. All around the world, people increasingly take advantage of what a global economy has to offer. They use VISA credit cards, wear Levi's jeans and Nike sneakers, consume Coca-Cola and McDonald's hamburgers, and communicate using Nokia phones or Dell computers. This is equally true for the buying habits of businesses. The market boundaries for IBM's services or GE's aircraft engines are no longer defined in political or geographic terms. Rather, it is the intrinsic value of these products and services that defines their appeal.

As the economies of the industrialized nations mature, growth prospects for many industries in traditional markets are diminishing. At the same time, other parts of the globe—for example, the Far East, central and eastern Europe, and Latin America—are experiencing faster economic development, causing the center of gravity of the world's business climate to swing from the developed economies to the developing nations. This shift in global economic activity is driven by many factors: Living standards in developing countries are rising, free enterprise is spreading across the globe, technology is advancing, barriers to trade are coming down, communication is becoming instantaneous worldwide, and global financial systems deliver capital efficiently to where it is used most productively.

Economic Globalization and Political Splintering

The positive aspects of globalization are well understood. Globalization has created millions of jobs from Thailand to Central America, brought telephone service to some 300 million households in developing nations, and transferred nearly $2 trillion from the West to poorer nations through direct investment. The opening of borders has allowed ideas and technology to flow freely around the globe, fueled productivity growth, and helped companies to become more competitive. In the years to come, instant universal access to knowledge through the Internet is widely expected to help narrow the current divide that separates the haves from the have-nots.

The deepening integration of the global economy has also unleashed a number of protests and counterpressures that have caught many people by surprise. There are at least five factors behind the current backlash:

1. *Insecurity.*   Despite record high levels of employment, thousands of people still lose their jobs every year as U.S. multinationals restructure their operations and transfer parts of the value-creation process overseas. Globalization is increasingly being blamed for this, especially by unions representing older workers in old-economy companies.
2. *Mistrust.*   Several large, multinational institutions are facing a growing credibility gap. Human rights groups charge, for example, that the International Monetary Fund and the World Bank tacitly support governments that condone unacceptable human rights practices.
3. *Policy.*   Environmentalists are worried that undemocratic decision-making processes are undermining national sovereignty on environmental matters, while unions fear that unregulated free trade allows unfair competition from countries that lack labor standards at the expense of jobs at home.
4. *Priorities.*   The environment, human rights, and labor standards have become key issues among young people. Governmental and corporate agendas are not seen to have responded well to these concerns.

5. *Technophobia.* Respect for science and innovation is coming under pressure as evidenced by the strong reactions against genetically modified food and the possibility of human cloning. To some, the word *progress* itself has become suspect, just as the term *globalization* has become associated with a lack of values.[2]

CHANGE IN THE INDUSTRY ENVIRONMENT

Changes in the industry environment often have a more immediate influence on a company's strategic position. The entrance of a new competitor, for example, or a major breakthrough in product or process technology, can radically alter the competitive balance in an industry. Analysis of the industry environment should therefore be focused on identifying forces of change that potentially have a major effect on the structure and the drivers of competition in an industry.

What Is an Industry?

When we speak of industries, we tend to think in terms of a group of companies or organizations that compete directly with each other in the marketplace. Though intuitive, the simplicity of this definition masks a complex issue. In many instances, there is more than one way in which an industry can be reasonably defined. Do makers of facsimile machines compete (1) with each other, (2) with manufacturers of personal computers and PDAs, telephone companies, the U.S. Postal Service, and overnight delivery companies, or (3) with both? Is competition primarily between products, companies, or networks of alliance partners? Should we therefore analyze rivalry at the business-unit level or at the corporate level? Should we distinguish between regional competition and global rivalry?

Abell and Hammond suggest defining industries along four dimensions: *products, types of customers, geography,* and *stages in the production-distribution pipeline.*[3] The first dimension—products—can be further broken down into two components: *functions* and *technologies. Function* refers to what the product or service does. Some cooking appliances merely cook. Others cook and roast. Still others fry, boil, or do all. It is important to note that functionality can be actual or perceived. Some over-the-counter remedies, for example, are positioned as cold relievers, whereas others are promoted as allergy medicines. This is as much a matter of positioning and perception as of actual functionality. *Technology* is a second distinguishing factor; some cooking appliances use gas whereas others are electric.

Defining an industry's boundaries requires the simultaneous consideration of all of these dimensions. In addition, it is important to distinguish between the *industry* a company competes in and the *market(s) it serves.* For example, a company might compete in the appliance industry but choose refrigerators as its served market. Figure 2-1 reflects these considerations. It depicts an industry as a collection of (adjacent) three-dimensional cells, each comprising a particular combination of functions/uses, technologies/materials, and types of customers. The task of defining an industry, therefore, consists of identifying a group of market cells thought to be most relevant to the strategic analysis at hand.

In the process of generating strategic alternatives, it is often useful to use multiple definitions. Assessing a company's growth potential, for example, might require the use

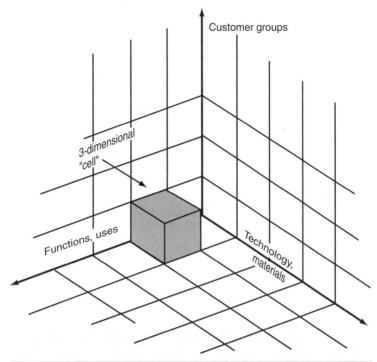

FIGURE 2-1   Dimensions of Industry Definition

Copyright © 1978 by the President and Fellows of Harvard College. Harvard
Business School Case 579-083. This case was prepared by Robert D. Buzzell as
the basis for class discussion rather than to illustrate either effective or
ineffective handling of an administrative situation. Reprinted by permission of
Harvard Business School.

of a different industry/market definition than, say, assessing its relative cost position.
The issue is one of scope.

Industry Structure and Porter's Five Forces Model

Michael Porter's *five forces model* is a useful tool for industry and competitive analysis.[4] It holds that an industry's profit potential is largely determined by the intensity of
the competitive rivalry within that industry, and that rivalry, in turn, is explained in
terms of five forces: *the threat of new entrants, the bargaining power of customers, the
bargaining power of suppliers, the threat of substitute products or services,* and *the jockeying among current rivals* (Figure 2-2).

The Threat of Entry

When it is relatively easy to enter a market, an industry can be expected to be
highly competitive. Potential new entrants threaten to increase the industry's capacity
and drive down prices and margins, to intensify the fight for market share and to upset
the balance between demand and supply. Whether this threat is real depends on two
factors: what barriers to entry exist and how entrenched competitors are likely to react.

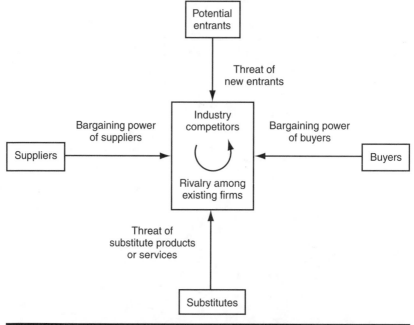

FIGURE 2-2 Porter's Five Forces Model

Source: Reprinted with the permission of The Free Press, an imprint of Simon & Schuster Adult Publishing Group, from *Competitive Strategy: Techniques for Analyzing Industries and Competitors* by Michael E. Porter. Copyright © 1980, 1998 by The Free Press.

There are six major barriers to market entry: economies of scale, product differentiation (brand equity), capital requirements, cost disadvantages independent of size, access to distribution channels, and government regulations. Consider, for example, the difficulty of entering the soft-drink industry and competing with advertising giants such as Coca-Cola and Pepsi, or the plight of microbrewers trying to gain distribution for their brands of beer against major companies such as Anheiser Busch. In high-technology industries, capital requirements and accumulated experience serve as major barriers. Industry conditions can change, however, and cause strategic windows of opportunity to open up. A prime example is deregulation. When airlines were deregulated in the early eighties, new carriers were able to enter the industry.

Powerful Suppliers and Buyers

Buyers and suppliers can sometimes influence the participants in an industry by exerting pressure over prices, quality, or the quantity demanded or sold. Consider, for example, how soft drink concentrate producers, by raising prices in the late eighties, contributed to the erosion of the profit margins of bottlers because those bottlers could not pass the increases on to the consumer.

Generally, suppliers are more powerful when (1) there are a few dominant companies and they are more concentrated than the industry they serve; (2) the component supplied is differentiated, making switching among suppliers difficult; (3) there are few substitutes; (4) suppliers can integrate forward; and (5) the industry comprises but a small portion of the suppliers' revenue base.

Buyers have substantial power when (1) there are few of them and/or they buy in large volume; (2) the product is relatively undifferentiated, making it easy to switch to other suppliers; (3) the buyers' purchases represent a sizable portion of the sellers' total revenues; and (4) buyers can integrate backward, among other factors. WalMart, for example, because of its size and industry position, has considerable leverage in negotiating with suppliers.

Substitute Products and Services

Substitute products and services continually threaten most industries and, in effect, place a lid on prices and profitability. HBO and pay-per-view are substitutes for the movie rental business and effectively limit what the industry can charge for its services. Moreover, if cost structures can be changed, for example, by employing new technology, substitutes can take substantial market share from existing businesses. The increased availability of pay-per-view entertainment over cable networks, for example, has begun to erode the competitive position of movie rental companies. From a strategic perspective, therefore, substitute products or services that deserve the closest scrutiny are those that (1) show improvements in price-performance relative to the industry average and (2) are produced by industries with deep pockets.

Rivalry Among Participants

How competitive an industry is also depends greatly on the number, relative size, and competitive prowess of its participants; the industry's growth rate; and related characteristics. Intense rivalry can be expected when (1) competitors are numerous and relatively equal in size and power, (2) industry growth is slow and the competitive battle is more about market share than creating new customers, (3) fixed costs are high or the product or service is perishable, (4) capacity increases can only be secured in large increments, and (5) exit barriers are high, making it expensive to discontinue operations.

Complementary Products — A Sixth Force?

Andrew Grove, founder of Intel, has suggested adding a sixth force to Porter's model: *the influence of complementary products*. Complementors are businesses from which customers buy complementary products. Computers need software, and software needs hardware; cars need gasoline, and gasoline needs service stations. When the interests of the industry are aligned with those of complementors, the status quo is preserved. New technologies or approaches can upset the existing order, however, and cause their paths to diverge.[5] An example is a change in technological standards, which renders previously compatible products and services incompatible.

The Influence of the Internet

The relative influence of these forces continues to shift as industry structures and business models change. Increasingly, companies are using the Internet to streamline their procurement of raw materials, components, and ancillary services. To the extent this enhances access to information about products and services and facilitates the valuation of alternate sources of supply, it increases the bargaining power of manufacturers over suppliers. However, the same technology might reduce barriers to entry for new suppliers and provide them with a direct channel to end users, thereby potentially reducing the leverage of intermediaries. The effect of the Internet on the possible threat of substitute products and services is equally ambiguous. On one hand, by increasing efficiency, it can expand markets. On the other hand, as new uses of the Internet are pioneered, the threat of substitutes might increase. At the same time, the Internet's rapid spread has reduced barriers to entry and increased rivalry among existing competitors in many industries. This has occurred because Internet-based business models generally are hard to protect from imitation and, because they often are focused on reducing variable costs, they sometimes create an unwanted focus on price. Thus, the Internet itself does not fundamentally alter the nature of the forces affecting industry rivalry. It can, however, change their relative influences on industry profitability and attractiveness.[6]

Strategic Groups

A *strategic group* is a set of firms that face similar threats and opportunities but different threats and opportunities than those faced by other sets of companies in the same industry. Rivalry is usually more intense within strategic groups than between them because members of the same strategic group focus on the same market segments with similar strategies and resources. In the fast-food industry, for example, hamburger chains tend to compete more directly with other hamburger chains than with chicken or pizza restaurants. Similarly, in pharmaceuticals, strategic groups can be defined in terms of what disease categories companies tend to focus on. Analysis of strategic groups helps explain how competition evolves within and between competitors with a similar strategic focus. Strategic groups can be mapped using broad characteristics, such as price, product-line breadth, degree of vertical integration, or other variables that differentiate competitors within an industry.

Industry Evolution

Industry structures change over time. Entry barriers may fall, as in the case of deregulation, or rise considerably, as has happened in a number of industries where brand identity became an important competitive weapon. Sometimes industries become more concentrated as real or perceived benefits of scale and scope cause businesses to consolidate. Models of *industry evolution* can help us understand how and why industries change over time. Perhaps the word *evolution* is somewhat deceptive; it suggests a process of slow, gradual change. Structural change can occur with remarkable rapidity, as in the case of deregulation or when a major technological breakthrough enhances the prospects of some companies at the expense of others.

The *product life cycle model*—based on the theory of diffusion of innovations and its logical counterpart, the pattern of acceptance of new ideas—is perhaps the best known model of industry evolution. It holds that an industry passes through a number of stages—introduction, growth, maturity, and decline—over time. The different stages are defined by changes in the rate of growth of industry sales, generally thought to follow an S-shaped curve reflecting the cumulative result of first and repeat adoptions of a product or service over time (Figure 2-3).

Though useful as a general construct for understanding how the principle of diffusion can shape industry sales over time, the product life cycle concept has little predictive value. Empirical studies have shown repeatedly that industry growth does not always

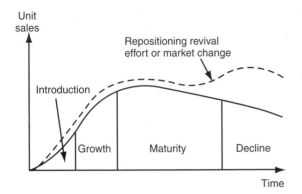

FIGURE 2-3   The Product Life Cycle Concept

Source: William M. Moore and Edgar A. Pessemier, *Product Planning and Management: Designing and Delivering Values.* Copyright © 1993 McGraw-Hill Company, Inc., New York, NY. Reproduced with permission.

follow an S-shaped pattern and that industries can be revived a number of times before declining. In some instances stages are skipped, whereas at other times they repeat themselves. More importantly, the product life cycle concept does not allow for the possibility that companies, through strategic actions such as increasing the pace of innovation or repositioning their offerings, can *affect* the shape of the growth curve. Taking an industry growth curve as a given, therefore, can become a self-fulfilling prophecy. We will discuss this model and its implications for strategy in greater detail in Chapter 4.

For analytic purposes, it is often useful to analyze changes in industry structure in terms of a number of key dimensions, such as the movement from a primarily *vertical* to a more *horizontal* structure or vice versa, changes in the degree of industry *concentration,* increases or decreases in the degree of *product differentiation,* and changes in the relative *maturity* of the industry.

These dimensions are illustrated by the convergence of three industries that originated some 50 years apart—telecommunications, computers, and television. This convergence has spawned a multimedia industry in which traditional industry boundaries have all but disappeared. Instead of consisting of three distinct businesses in which being vertically integrated was key to success, the industry has evolved into five primarily horizontal segments: content (products and services), packaging (bundling of content and additional functionality), network (physical infrastructure), transmission (distribution), and display devices. In this new structure, strategic advantage for many companies is primarily determined by their relative positions within one of the five segments. Vertical integration is widely expected to become an important strategy once again when economies of scale and scope become more critical to competitive success and a principal driver behind another round of industry consolidation; industry evolution can move in cycles.

When economies of scale are important and market share and total unit cost are inversely related, industry structures are often more *concentrated.* In such industries the size distribution of business firms is often highly skewed and the so-called "Rule of Three and Four" may apply. This rule states that many stable markets will have only three significant competitors, and that the market shares of these competitors will roughly be proportioned as four-to-two-to-one. Studies have also shown that, as markets mature, they sometimes become less concentrated, suggesting that the relationship between relative share and cost position is less pronounced for *mature* markets than it is for *immature* markets. The latter explains why larger companies often lose market share as the industry matures: Their cost advantage diminishes over time. In contrast, in *fragmented* industries, characterized by a relatively *low degree of concentration,* no single player has a major market share. Such industries are found in many areas of the economy. Some are highly *differentiated,* such as application software; others tend toward *commodity* status, as in the case of lumber. In the absence of major forces for change, fragmented industries can remain fragmented for a long time.

New Patterns

Many new industries, such as cellular telephone or high-definition television, cannot evolve without some convergence in technological standards. Competition for standards or formats is frequently waged by a group of companies led by the developer of one standard competing with another group of companies favoring a different standard. Competition for standard or format share is important because the winning standard will garner its promoters a substantial share of future profits. The current battle for standards for cell phone technologies and set-top boxes, for example, might well decide the ultimate winners in the race for market share.

For industries in which competition for standards has become an important determinant of strategic success, Prahalad has proposed a new model that describes industry evolution in three phases.[7] In the first phase, competition is mostly focused on *ideas, product concepts, technology choices,* and *the building of a competency base.* The primary goal at this stage is to learn more about the potential of the industry and about the key factors that will determine future success or failure. In the second phase, competition is more about *building a viable coalition of partners that will support a standard against competing formats.* Companies cooperating at this stage may compete vigorously in phase three of the process—*the battle for market share for end products and profits.*

As competition becomes more global, industries consolidate and technology becomes more pervasive, the lines between customers, suppliers, competitors, and partners are increasingly becoming blurred. With greater frequency companies that compete in one market collaborate in others. At times, they can be each other's customers or suppliers. This complex juxtaposition of roles suggests that questions such as "What will this industry look like in five or ten years' time?" are often extremely difficult to answer and that relying on simple, stylized models of industry evolution can be dangerous. As industry boundaries become more permeable, structural changes in *adjacent* industries (industries serving the same customer base with different products or services, or industries using similar technologies and production processes) or *related* industries (industries supplying components, technologies, or complementary services) increasingly influence an industry's outlook for the future. Finally, change sometimes is simply a function of time. For example, buyers generally become more discriminating as they become more familiar with a product and its substitutes and, as a consequence, are likely to be more explicit in their demands.

Deregulation or Reregulation?

Deregulation continues to redefine the competitive landscape in many industries. In the United States, first the airline and telecommunications industries, and more recently the financial services and energy industries, experienced major changes as barriers to entry were brought down, competition heated up, and upstarts challenged the existing order. As more industries are deregulated, competitive behavior will come under greater scrutiny, at home as well as abroad. Whereas antitrust once was primarily a domestic issue adjudicated by the Federal Trade Commission or the Justice Department, today regulatory authorities from other parts of the world, such as the European Union, are deeply involved. In the process, the regulatory focus is shifting from simple measures of local concentration to one of promoting competition, protecting consumers, and preserving innovation on a global basis.

RISK AND UNCERTAINTY

Many strategic choices involve future events that are difficult to predict. The success of a new product introduction, for example, can depend on such factors as how current and potential competitors will react, the quality of components procured from outside suppliers, and the state of the economy. To capture the lack of predictability, decision-making situations are often described along a continuum of states ranging from *certainty* to *risk* to *uncertainty*. Under conditions of certainty, accurate, measurable information is available about the outcome of each alternative considered. When an event is risky, we cannot predict its outcome with certainty but have enough information to assess its probability. Under conditions of uncertainty, little is known about the alternatives or their outcomes.

To make analysis of the strategic environment actionable, we must be able to assess the degree of *uncertainty* associated with relevant events, the *speed* with which changes are likely to occur, as well as the possible *outcomes* they foreshadow. Conditions of certainty and risk lend themselves to formal analysis; uncertainty presents unique problems. Some change takes place gradually and is knowable if not predictable. We might not be able to determine exactly when and how they affect a specific industry or issue, but their broad effect is relatively well understood. The globalization of the competitive climate and most demographic and social trends fall into this category. The prospect of new industry regulations creates a more immediate kind of uncertainty—the new regulatory structure will either be adopted or it will not. The collapse of boundaries between industries constitutes yet another scenario: The change forces themselves may be identifiable, but their outcomes may not be totally predictable. Finally, there are change forces, such as the sudden collapse of foreign governments, outbreaks of war, or major technological discoveries, that are inherently random in nature and cannot easily be foreseen.

The Concept of a Change Arena

The concept of a change arena is useful in describing the different levels of uncertainty associated with a particular strategic challenge. A *change arena* is a pictorial representation of the relative strength of strategic forces of change and forces of resistance in terms of four domains (Figure 2-4):[8]

- *Domain 1: Weak change forces, strong resistance.*   Many stable or highly regulated industries are somewhat sheltered from radical change and controlled by a few dominant firms with the lion's share of the market. The salt and paint industries provide good examples. In these industries, strategic positions are

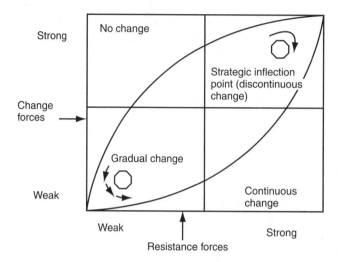

FIGURE 2-4 The Concept of a Change Arena

Copyright © 1994, by The Regents of the University of California. Reprinted from the *California Management Review,* vol. 36, no. 2. By permission of The Regents.

generally well understood by all players and tend to be fairly stable over time. As long as resistance forces dominate the forces for change, strategic behavior will be highly predictable—its essence is continuity. Provided the strength of the change forces does not increase, this situation can last indefinitely.

- *Domain 2: Strong change forces, weak resistance.* When the forces of change far exceed the threshold of resistance and change occurs continuously, no individual player or even a small group of players can block the forces of change. A number of high-technology industries, such as software, populated by a larger number of small, innovative players, share this trait of continuous adaptation.

- *Domain 3: Weak change forces, weak resistance.* Industries with weak but finely balanced forces of change and resistance tend to experience sporadic, relatively minor turning points when the balance is upset by events such as the occasional entry of a new competitor, relatively minor changes in technology, or small shifts in economic conditions. On the whole, the industry and the companies that comprise the industry adapt relatively easily to the new conditions, and the fundamentals that determine industry behavior remain intact. A number of retailing sectors fit this profile.

- *Domain 4: Strong change forces, strong resistance.* When strong change forces duel with strong forces of resistance, change can be sharply discontinuous. Think of the impact of the invention of the semiconductor or of events such as deregulation in the airline and telecommunications industries. Such shocks to the system are characterized by a massive shift from the status quo to a new order. Such upheavals are often called *strategic inflection points.* Strategic inflection points are relatively rare in most industries, but when they occur their consequence is substantial. They are not confined to high-technology environments. The advent of privatization, for example, defined a strategic inflection point in the former communist world. Anticipating strategic inflection points and capitalizing on the opportunities they represent are two of the greatest challenges in strategy development.

The *strength* of a change force (or counter force)—whether it originates within or outside a company—is determined by the change's current and future effect on a firm's competitive position. A strong change force can substantially erode a company's market position if the company does not anticipate, prepare, and respond appropriately to it at the right time. On the other hand, observant companies have an opportunity to strengthen their competitive positions by leveraging the momentum generated by the change force. Consider the shift from mainframe to distributed computing. A number of companies, including IBM, substantially underestimated the strength or timing of this change force and saw their competitive position (temporarily) eroded. Meanwhile, a number of startup firms carefully staked out a position in the distributed computing arena or simply were in the right position at the right time. Whether by chance or design, their positioning created the opportunity to ride the wave of this change force to prosperity.

Scenario Analysis

Originally developed at Royal Dutch/Shell in London, *scenario analysis* is one of the most widely used techniques for constructing alternative plausible futures of a business's external environment. Its purpose is to analyze the effects of various uncontrollable change forces on the strategic playing field and to test the resiliency of specific strategy alternatives. It is most heavily used by businesses that are highly sensitive to external forces, such as energy companies.

Scenario analysis is a disciplined method for imagining and examining possible futures.[9] It divides knowledge into two categories: things we believe we know something about and elements we consider uncertain or unknowable. The first mainly focuses on the forward projection of knowable change forces. For example, we can safely make assumptions about demographic shifts or the substitution effects of new technologies. Obvious examples of uncertain aspects—the second category—are future interest rates, oil prices, results of political elections, and rates of innovation. Since scenarios depict possible futures but not specific strategies to deal with them, it makes sense to invite outsiders into the process, such as major customers, key suppliers, regulators, consultants, and academics. The objective is to see the future broadly in terms of fundamental trends and uncertainties and to build a shared framework for strategic thinking that encourages diversity and sharper perceptions about external changes and opportunities.

Scenario planning differs from other planning methods, such as contingency planning, sensitivity analysis, and computer simulation, in three major ways:

1. Contingency planning examines only one uncertainty, such as "What if we don't get FDA approval for our drug?" It presents a base case and an exception or contingency. Scenario analysis explores the joint impact of various uncertainties.

2. Sensitivity analysis examines the effect of a change in one variable, keeping all other variables constant. Scenario analysis, on the other hand, allows for changing several variables at a time. Scenario analysis focuses on capturing the new states that will develop after major shocks or deviations in key variables occur.

3. Scenarios are more than just the output of a complex simulation model. They often include elements that were not or cannot be formally modeled, such as new regulations, value shifts, or innovations. Hence, scenario analysis goes beyond objective analysis to include subjective interpretations.

The process for developing scenarios involves four principal steps:

1. Deciding what possible future developments to probe, which trends—technological change, demographic trends, or resource issues—to include, and what time horizon is to be considered.
2. Identifying what forces or developments likely have the greatest ability to shape the future.
3. Constructing a comprehensive set of future scenarios based on different combinations of possible outcomes. Some combinations will be of greater interest than others, either because they have a greater effect on the strategic issue at hand or because they are more or less likely to occur. As a result, a few scenarios usually emerge that become the focus of a more-detailed analysis.
4. Generating scenario-specific forecasts that allow an assessment of the implications of the alternative futures for strategic postures and choices.

The final set of scenarios analyzed should have four qualities:

1. *Relevance.* To have impact, the different scenarios should connect directly with the mental maps and concerns of the users (e.g., senior executives, middle managers, etc.).
2. *Consistency.* The scenarios should be internally consistent.
3. *Descriptiveness.* Scenarios should describe generically different futures rather than variations on one theme.
4. *Actionability.* Ideally, each scenario should describe an equilibrium or a state in which the system might exist for some length of time, as opposed to being highly transient. It does an organization little good to prepare for a possible future that will be quite short-lived.

Uncertainty and Strategy

In characterizing how firms deal with uncertainty, Courtney et al. distinguish among *shapers, adapters,* and *companies reserving the right to play.*[10]

Shapers are proactive. They drive an industry toward a structure that is to their benefit. They are out to change the rules of the competitive game and to try to control the direction of the market. An example is Kodak's attempt to fundamentally change the way people create, store, and view pictures with its new digital photography.

Adapters exhibit a more reactive posture. They take the current industry structure as a given and often bet on gradual, evolutionary change. In strategic environments characterized by relatively low levels of uncertainty, adapters position themselves for competitive advantage within the current structure. At higher levels of uncertainty, they may behave more cautiously and fine-tune their abilities to react quickly to new developments.

The third posture, also reactive in nature, *reserves the right to play.* Companies pursuing this posture often make incremental investments to preserve their options until the strategic environment becomes easier to read or less uncertain. Making partial investments in competing technologies, taking a small equity position in different startup companies, or experimenting with different distribution options are examples of reserving the right to play.

NOTES

1. Peter F. Drucker, *Management Challenges for the 21st Century,* HarperBusiness, 1999, Chapter 2, p. 43 on.
2. "What's behind the global backlash?" *Business Week,* April 24, 2000, p. 202.
3. Derek Abell and John Hammond, *Strategic Market Planning: Problems and Analytical Approaches,* Prentice Hall, 1979.
4. Michael Porter, *Competitive Strategy,* Free Press, 1980.
5. Andrew S. Grove, *Only the Paranoid Survive,* Doubleday, 1996.
6. Michael E. Porter, "Strategy and the Internet," *Harvard Business Review,* March 2001, pp. 63–78.
7. C. K. Prahalad, "Weak signals versus strong paradigms," *Journal of Marketing Research,* Vol. 32, 1995, pp. iii–ix.
8. This categorization is based on Paul Strebel, "Choosing the Right Change Path," *California Management Review,* Vol. 36, No. 2, Winter 1994, pp. 29–51.
9. The following description is based on P. J. H. Schoemaker and C. A. J. M. van de Heijden, "Integrating Scenarios into Strategic Planning at Royal Dutch/Shell," *Planning Review,* Vol. 20, 1992, pp. 41–46.
10. Hugh Courtney, Jane Kirkland, and Patrick Viguerie, "Strategy Under Uncertainty," *Harvard Business Review,* Nov./Dec. 1997, pp. 66–79.

CHAPTER

3

Leveraging Internal Resources and Change Drivers for Competitive Advantage

INTRODUCTION

Analysis of external forces is valuable in determining the strategic changes a company *should* consider. However, an assessment of internal strategic resources and capabilities—and of pressures for and against change—is critical when determining what strategies a company successfully *can* pursue. A firm's strategic resources include its physical assets; its relative financial position; the quality of its people; and specific knowledge, competencies, processes, skills, and cultural aspects of the organization. Pressures for strategic change by internal forces or a firm's immediate stakeholders emanate from persistently disappointing performance, new owners or management, limitations to growth using current strategies, scarcity of critical resources, and internal cultural changes.

Analyzing a company's internal strategic environment, therefore, has two principal components: (1) cataloging and valuing current resources and core competencies that can be used to create a competitive advantage and (2) identifying internal pressures for change and forces of resistance.

This chapter consists of four parts. In the first part, we characterize a company's strategic resource base in terms of physical, financial, human resource, and organizational assets, and describe techniques for analyzing a company's strategic resource base. In the second section, we focus on the relationship between a company's strategic resources and competitive advantage, and introduce value chain analysis. Third, we discuss internal organizational change drivers and counterforces that have a major influence on the feasibility of exercising particular strategic options, and we introduce the company life cycle model. In the final section, we look at two analysis frameworks—the Balanced Scorecard, and SWOT analysis—that are useful for diagnosing, assessing, and summarizing a company's overall current strategic position and need and readiness for strategic change.

STRATEGIC RESOURCES

A company's strategic resource base consists of its *physical, financial, human resource*, and *organizational assets*. Physical assets such as state-of-the-art manufacturing facilities or plant or service locations near important customers can materially affect a company's competitiveness. Financial strength—excellent cash flow, a strong balance sheet, and a strong financial track record—is a measure of a company's competitive position, market success, and ability to invest in its future. The quality of a company's human resources—strong leadership at the top, experienced managers, and well-trained, motivated employees—may well be a firm's most important strategic resource. Finally, strategic organizational resources are the specific competencies, processes, skills, and knowledge under the control of a corporation. They include such qualities as a firm's manufacturing experience, brand equity, innovativeness, relative cost position, and ability to adapt and learn as circumstances change.

To evaluate the relative worth of a company's strategic resources, four specific questions should be asked: (1) How valuable is a resource; does it help build and sustain competitive advantage? (2) Is this a unique resource or do other competitors have similar resources? If competitors have substantially similar resources or capabilities or can obtain them with relative ease, their strategic value is diminished. (3) Is the strategic resource easy to imitate? This is related to uniqueness. Ultimately, most strategic resources, with the exception of patents and trademarks, can be duplicated. The question is—At what cost? The more expensive it is for rivals to duplicate a strategic resource, the more valuable it is to a company. (4) Is the company positioned to exploit the resource? Possessing a strategic resource is one thing; being able to exploit it is quite another. A strategic resource that has little value to one company might be an important strategic asset for another. The issue is whether a resource can be leveraged for competitive advantage.

Physical Assets

A company's physical assets, such as state-of-the-art manufacturing facilities and plant or service locations near important customers, can materially affect a company's competitiveness. For airline companies, the average age of their fleet of aircraft is an important concern; it affects customer perceptions, routing flexibility, and operating and maintenance costs. Infrastructure is a key issue for telecommunications companies; it determines their geographical reach and defines the types of customer service they can provide. In retailing and real estate, the old adage "location, location, location" still applies.

Physical assets do not necessarily need to be owned. Judicious use of options such as leasing, franchising, and partnering can substantially enhance a company's reach with a relatively modest commitment of resources.

Analyzing a Company's Financial Resource Base

At the corporate level, an evaluation of a company's financial performance and position involves a thorough analysis of the company's *income statement, balance sheet,* and *cash flows.* At the divisional or business unit level, such an evaluation is usually limited to an analysis of the income and cash flow statements.

Financial Ratio Analysis can provide a quick overview of a company's or business unit's current or past profitability, liquidity, leverage, and activity. *Profitability ratios* measure how well a company is allocating its resources. *Liquidity ratios* focus on cash flow generation and a company's ability to meet its financial obligations. *Leverage ratios* may suggest potential improvements in the financing of operations. *Activity ratios* measure productivity and efficiency. Such ratios (Figure 3-1) can be used to assess (1) the business's position in the industry, (2) the degree to which certain

FIGURE 3-1   Ratio Analysis

	Ratio	*Definition*
1. Profitability		
a. Gross profit margin:	$\dfrac{\text{sales} - \text{cost of goods sold}}{\text{sales}}$	Total margin available to cover operating expenses and yield a profit
b. Net profit margin:	$\dfrac{\text{profits after taxes}}{\text{sales}}$	Return on sales
c. Return on assets:	$\dfrac{\text{earnings before interest and taxes (EBIT)}}{\text{total assets}}$	Return on the total investment from both stockholders and creditors
d. Return on equity:	$\dfrac{\text{profits after taxes}}{\text{total equity}}$	Rate of return on stockholders' investment in the firm
2. Liquidity		
a. Current ratio:	$\dfrac{\text{current assets}}{\text{current liabilities}}$	The extent to which the claims of short-term creditors are covered by short-term assets
b. Quick ratio:	$\dfrac{\text{current assets} - \text{inventory}}{\text{current liabilities}}$	Acid-test ratio; the firm's ability to pay off short-term obligations without having to sell its inventory
c. Inventory to net working capital:	$\dfrac{\text{inventory}}{\text{current assets} - \text{current liabilities}}$	The extent to which the firm's working capital is tied up in inventory
3. Leverage		
a. Debt-to-assets ratio:	$\dfrac{\text{total debt}}{\text{total assets}}$	The extent to which borrowed funds are used to finance the firm's operations
b. Debt-to-equity ratio:	$\dfrac{\text{total debt}}{\text{total equity}}$	Ratio of funds from creditors to funds from stockholders
c. Long-term debt-to-equity ratio:	$\dfrac{\text{long-term debt}}{\text{total equity}}$	The balance between debt and equity
4. Activity		
a. Inventory turnover:	$\dfrac{\text{sales}}{\text{inventory}}$	The amount of inventory used by the company to generate its sales
b. Fixed-asset turnover:	$\dfrac{\text{sales}}{\text{fixed assets}}$	Sales productivity and plant utilization
c. Average collection:	$\dfrac{\text{accounts receivable}}{\text{average daily sales}}$	The average length of time required to receive payment

strategic objectives are being attained, (3) the business's vulnerability to revenue and cost swings, and (4) the level of financial risk associated with the current (or proposed) strategy.

The *DuPont* formula for analyzing a company's or business unit's return on assets directly links operating variables to financial performance. For example, as shown in Figure 3-2, return on assets is computed by multiplying earnings, expressed as a percentage of sales, by asset turnover. Asset turnover, in turn, is the ratio of sales to total assets employed. A careful analysis of such relationships allows pointed questions about a strategy's effectiveness and the quality of its execution.

Accounting-based measures have generally been found to be inadequate indicators of a business unit's economic value. *Shareholder value analysis,* in contrast, focuses on cash flow generation, which is the principal determinant of shareholder wealth. It is helpful in answering such questions as (1) Does the current strategic plan create shareholder value, and, if so, how much? (2) How does the business unit's performance compare to the performance of others in the corporation? and (3) Would an alternative strategy increase shareholder value more than the current strategy?

FIGURE 3-2 The DuPont Formula for Computing Return on Assets

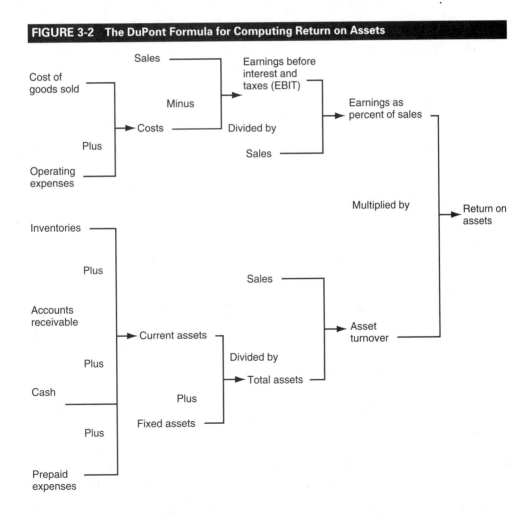

Simple, accounting-based financial measures used to assess current performance, such as return on investment (ROI), have been replaced by broader shareholder value-based measures such as *economic value added* (EVA) and *market value added* (MVA). EVA is a value-based financial performance measure that focuses on economic value creation. Unlike traditional measures based on accounting profit, EVA recognizes that capital has two components: the cost of debt and the cost of equity. Most traditional measures such as return on assets (ROA) and return on equity (ROE) focus on the cost of debt but ignore the cost of equity. The premise of EVA is that executives cannot know whether an operation is really creating value until they assess the complete cost of capital.

In mathematical terms, EVA = Profit − [(Cost of Capital)(Total Capital)], where *profit* is after-tax operating profit, *cost of capital* is the weighted cost of debt and equity, and *total capital* is book value plus interest-bearing debt. Consider the following example. When buying an asset, executives invest capital from their company and borrowed funds from a lender. Both the stockholders and the lender require a return on their capital. This return is the *cost of capital* and includes both the cost of equity (the company's investment) and the cost of debt (the lender's investment). The company does not generate any meaningful profits until returns generated by the investment exceed the weighted capital charge. Once this occurs, the assets are contributing a positive EVA. If, on the other hand, the returns continue to lag the weighted cost of capital, EVA is negative, and change may be needed.

Variety, Inc. used EVA as a basis for reinvigorating its corporate culture and reestablishing its financial health. The company focused employees' attention on its negative $150 million EVA position. It established clear objectives to turn EVA positive within a five-year time frame. These objectives included revising the firm's capital structure by initiating a stock buyback program, selectively evaluating strategic opportunities, and efficiently managing working capital. By establishing a 20 percent internal cost of capital, managers screened new strategic opportunities such as constructing a new manufacturing facility, establishing an Asian presence through a joint venture, and divesting its door-lock actuator business.[1]

Two additional benefits of EVA are that (1) it can help align employee and owner interests through employee compensation plans and (2) it can be used as the basis for a single competitive performance measure called *market value added* (MVA). Under EVA-based incentive programs, employees are rewarded for contributing to profits through the efficient use of capital. As employees become conscious of the results of their capital utilization decisions, they become more selective in the ways they spend shareholder investment. MVA is equal to market value less capital invested. Thus, EVA can be used as a metric for various internal functions such as capital budgeting, employee performance evaluation, and operational assessment. On the other hand, external shareholder value is measured through MVA, which is equal to future discounted EVA streams.

Although these are attractive features, effectively implementing EVA has proven difficult. What is more, several independent studies have produced mixed results regarding a relationship between EVA and superior firm performance.[2] In 1998, *Fortune* magazine reported that companies that used EVA posted average annual returns of 22%, versus 13% for competitors that did not use EVA.[3] The *Wall Street Journal,* on the other hand, referenced a study conducted at the University of Washington that concluded that "earnings per share (EPS) is still a more reliable guide to stock performance than EVA and other 'residual-income' measures."[4] Additionally, a study of 88 companies concluded that EVA adopters tend to emphasize financial measures over quality and customer service.[5] The findings further suggest that although initial performance gains are realized by EVA adopters, these improvements tend to stall shortly after EVA is implemented. It appears that for every study showing positive results for EVA, there is another study that is not supportive.

These reservations notwithstanding, EVA portrays the true results of a company by considering the cost of debt and equity. Tools such as ROE, ROA, and EPS measure financial performance but ignore the cost-of-equity component of cost of capital. Therefore, it is possible to have positive earnings and positive returns but a negative EVA. By encouraging an operation to minimize indebtedness, a firm that uses EVA maximizes capital efficiency and allocation. If, for example, a business can conserve its assets by improving collections of receivables and inventory turnover, EVA will rise.

Cost analysis deals with the identification of strategic cost drivers—those cost factors in the value chain that determine long-term competitiveness in the industry. Strategic cost drivers can include such variables as product design, factor costs, scale and scope of operations, and capacity utilization. To assist in strategy development, cost analysis should focus on those costs and cost drivers that are of strategic importance, i.e., those that can be influenced by strategic choice.

Cost benchmarking is useful for assessing a firm's costs relative to those of competing firms, or for comparing a company's performance against best-in-class companies. The process involves five steps: (1) selecting areas or operations to benchmark, (2) identifying key performance measures and practices, (3) identifying best-in-class companies or key competitors, (4) collecting cost and performance data, and (5) analyzing and interpreting the results. This technique is extremely practical and versatile. It allows for direct comparisons of the efficiencies with which different tasks in the value chain are performed. It is dangerous, however, to rely heavily on benchmarking for guidance because it focuses on similarities rather than differences between rival firms' strategic designs.

A complete evaluation of a company's financial resources should include a *financial risk* analysis. Most financial models are essentially deterministic. That is, managers specify a single estimate for each key variable. Yet, many of these estimates are made recognizing that there is a great deal of uncertainty about their true value. Together, such uncertainties can mask high levels of risk. It is important, therefore, that risk be explicitly considered. This involves determining which variables have the greatest effect on revenues and costs as a basis for assessing different risk scenarios. Some of the variables that are commonly considered are market growth rate, market share, price trends, the cost of capital, and the useful life of the underlying technology.

Human Capital: A Company's Most Valuable Strategic Resource

Companies are run by and for people. Although some strategic resources can be duplicated, the people who make up an organization or its immediate stakeholders are unique. Understanding their concerns, aspirations, and capabilities is therefore key to determining a company's strategic position and options.

A survey by *Chief Executive* magazine in 2001 demonstrates that more and more focus is being put on attracting, developing, and retaining *human capital*. Of the CEOs surveyed, 43 percent believe that finding and retaining good people are their greatest challenges, and 84 percent believe people issues are far more important than they were three years ago. A study conducted by the American Society for Training and Development examined 500 U.S.-based publicly traded firms. Looking at annual training expenditures and stockholder returns, it concluded that the top half of firms in terms of spending on training had higher stockholder returns than did the bottom half.[6]

Continuous employee development, through on-the-job training and other programs, is critical to the growth of human capital. FedEx develops its homegrown talent through a commitment to continuous learning. The company puts 3 percent of its total expenses into training, six times the proportion of the average company. Both line staff and managers attend 11 weeks of mandatory training in their first year. More than 10,000 employees have been to the Leadership Institute and have attended weeklong courses on the company's culture and operations.[7] Many other companies are adopting similar strategies and reaping the benefits. Motorola executives report that their company receives $33 for every $1 invested in employee education.

Organizational Strategic Resources

A firm's organizational resources include its *knowledge and intellectual capital base;* its *reputation* with customers, partners, suppliers, and the financial community; specific *competencies, processes, and skill sets;* and its *corporate culture.*

Knowledge and intellectual capital are major drivers of competitive advantage. A firm's competitive advantage comes from the value it delivers to customers. Competitive advantage is created and sustained when companies continue to mobilize new knowledge faster and more efficiently than their competitors. Recognizing the importance of knowledge as a strategic asset, Skandia, Nasdaq, Chevron, and Dow Chemical have established director-level positions in charge of intellectual capital.

Additional evidence of the growing importance of knowledge and intellectual capital as strategic resources is provided by the financial markets. Although intellectual capital is difficult to measure and not formally represented on the balance sheet, a company's market capitalization increasingly reflects the value of such resources and the effectiveness with which they are managed. Netscape, before being acquired, had a $4 billion market capitalization based on its stock price, even though the company's sales were only a few million dollars per year. Investors based the high stock price on their assessment of the company's intangibles—its knowledge base and quality of management.

The number of *patents* issued in America each year has doubled in the last decade. In Europe, the growth has been slower, largely because patents are harder to secure. Increasingly, patents are global, however. Through a new international patent system organized by the United Nations World Intellectual Property Organization, through the World Trade Organization, and through growing demand from inventors for patents that are protected throughout the world, patenting systems are slowly converging. Landmark court decisions also have made new areas of technology patentable in the United States. A 1980 case opened biotechnology and genes for patenting, a 1981 case allowed the patenting of software, and a 1998 case spawned more business-method patents.

Strong patent protection can be of great strategic value. For example, to protect its intellectual property and preserve its competitive advantage in the manufacturing and testing processes involved in its build-to-order system, Dell Computer secured 77 patents protecting different parts of the building and testing process. Such protection pays. IBM collected $30 million in a patent-infringement suit from Microsoft—after which Bill Gates sent a memo to employees with the directive to "patent as much as we can."

Increasingly, patents are exploited strategically to generate addditional revenues. Licensing patents has helped build the market for IBM technology and boosted its licensing revenues from $500 million in 1994 to $1.5 billion in 1999, about one-fifth of the company's profits. An increasing number of firms practice *strategic patenting*—using patent applications to colonize entire new areas of technology even before tangible products are created.

Service companies are beginning to use patents offensively. Applications from financial-services companies to protect the design of new financial-services products are increasing, and some of the major accounting firms are considering submitting patent applications for their consulting processes. Walker Digital, an Internet company, has at least 12 patents and another 200 applications in the pipeline. One of them deals with reverse auctions, in which customers set a price they are willing to pay and airlines and other suppliers decide whether to meet it. That patent spawned Priceline.com, Cheaptickets.com, and Expedia.com.

The largest part of a company's intellectual capital base, however, is not patentable. It represents the total *knowledge* accumulated by individuals, groups, and units within an organization about customers, suppliers, products, and processes, and is made up of a mixture of past experiences, values, education, and insights. As an organization learns, it makes better decisions. Better decisions, in turn, improve performance and enhance learning.

Knowledge becomes an asset when it is managed and transferred. *Explicit* knowledge is formal and objective and can be codified and stored in books, archives, and databases. *Implicit* or *tacit* knowledge is informal and subjective. It is gained through experience and transferred through personal interaction and collaboration. A study about how Xerox repair technicians refined their knowledge illustrates the difference.[8] The company's assumption had been that the technicians serviced companies' copying machines by following the documented diagnostic road maps that Xerox provided. Research, however, revealed that technicians often went to breakfast together, and while eating, talked about their work. They exchanged stories, posed problems, offered solutions, constructed answers, and discussed the machines, thereby keeping one another up to date about what they had learned. What was thought to be a process based on explicit knowledge in fact was based on tacit knowledge, experience, and collaboration.[9]

To effectively develop knowledge as an asset, a company must encourage individual and organizational learning, knowledge creation, codification, and sharing. It also must combat the "knowledge is power" syndrome and identify and eliminate disincentives to knowledge-sharing through changes in incentives, accountability, and corporate culture. Nucor's cash incentives to employees to contribute their knowledge were so high that in the 1990s the payouts for production employees averaged 80 to 150 percent of base wages, with no upper limit.[10]

A firm's *reputation*—with customers, partners, suppliers, and regulatory agencies—can be a powerful strategic asset. Physical distance between customers, distributors, and manufacturers created the need for *brands* in the 19th century. They provided a guarantee of reliability and quality. In a global and Internet-based economy, they build trust and reinforce value. Consumers might be reluctant to use their credit cards to purchase products over the Internet if it were not for the trust they accord to companies such as Amazon, Dell, or eBay. Because consumer trust is the basis of all brand values, companies that own the brands have an immense incentive to work to retain that trust.

Thus, *brands* are strategic assets that assist companies in building and retaining customer loyalty. A strong brand can help maintain profit margins and erect barriers to entry. Because a brand is so valuable to a company, it must constantly be nourished, sustained, and protected. Doing so is becoming harder and more expensive. Consumers are busier, are more distracted, and have more media options than ever before. Coca-Cola, Gillette, and Nike struggle to increase volumes, raise prices, and boost margins. What is more, failure in support of a brand can be catastrophic. A mistargeted advertising campaign, a drop-off in quality, or a corporate scandal can quickly reduce the value of a brand and the reputation of the company that owns it.

Core Competencies

Core competencies represent unique capabilities that allow a company to build a competitive advantage. 3M has developed a core competency in coatings. Canon has core competencies in optics, imaging, and microprocessor controls. Procter & Gamble's marketing prowess allows it to adapt more quickly than its rivals to changing opportunities. The development of core competencies has become a key element in building a long-term strategic advantage. An assessment of strategic resources and capabilities, therefore, must include assessments of the core competencies a company has or is developing, how they are nurtured, and how they can be leveraged.

Core competencies evolve as a firm develops its business processes and incorporates its intellectual assets. Core competencies are not just things a company does particularly well; rather, they represent sets of skills or systems that create a uniquely high value for customers at best-in-class levels.[11] To qualify, such skills or systems should contribute to perceived customer benefits, be difficult for competitors to imitate, and allow for leverage across markets. Honda's use of small-engine technology in a variety of products—including motorcycles, jet skis, and lawn mowers—is a good example.

Core competencies should be focused on creating value and be adapted as customer requirements change. Targeting a carefully selected set of core competencies also benefits innovation. Charles Schwab, for example, successfully leveraged its core competency in brokerage services by expanding its client communication methods to include the Internet and financial advisors.

Hamel and Prahalad suggest three tests for identifying core competencies. First, core competencies should provide access to a broad array of markets. Second, core competencies should help differentiate core products and services. Third, core competencies should be hard to imitate because they represent multiple skills, technologies, and organizational elements.[12]

Experience shows that only a few companies have the resources to develop more than a handful of core competencies. Picking the right ones, therefore, is the key. "Which resources or capabilities should we keep in-house and develop into core competencies and which ones should we outsource?" is a key question to ask. Pharmaceutical companies, for example, increasingly outsource clinical testing in an effort to focus their resource base on drug development. Generally, the development of core competencies should focus on long-term platforms capable of adapting to new market circumstances; on unique sources of leverage in the value chain; on areas where the firm thinks it can dominate; on elements that are important to customers in the long run; and on key skills and knowledge, not on products.

Corporate Culture

Performance is linked to the strength of a company's corporate culture. Common elements of strong culture include leaders who demonstrate strong values that are aligned with the competitive conditions; a company commitment to operating under pervasive principles that are not easily abandoned; and a concern for employees, customers, and shareholders. Conversely, below-average profit performance is associated with weak corporate cultures. Employees in these cultures report experiencing separateness from the organization, the development of fiefdoms, the prevalence of political maneuvering, and hostility toward change.

A company's *corporate culture* is a shared system of values, assumptions, and beliefs among a firm's employees that provides guidance on how to think, perceive, and act. Because of its pronounced effect on employee behavior and effectiveness, companies increasingly recognize that corporate culture can set them apart from competitors. At United Parcel Service (UPS), for instance, culture is considered a strategic asset, ever growing in importance: "Managing that culture to competitive advantage involves three key priorities: recruiting and retaining the right people, nurturing innovation, and building a customer mind-set."[13] UPS executives believe that the firm's culture is so important that the company spends more than $300 million annually on employee training and education programs, with a great deal of the expenditures involving the introduction of the company's culture to new employees.

In every organization, employees acquire a set of shared assumptions as they solve problems. Because these assumptions have resulted from past success, they gain validity. They are subsequently taught to new employees as the correct way to think about problem-solving.[14] Southwest Airlines' executives have three basic values that they promote throughout the company as a means to developing a desirable corporate culture: work should be fun, work is important, and people are important. To build and maintain this culture, peers are responsible for choosing new hires. The hiring process uses formal applications, phone-screening interviews, group interviews, interviews with individual employees, consensus assessments, and votes.[15] Using this process, Southwest has created a culture that materially improves performance; it has been able to maintain an unequalled level of customer satisfaction in the industry. The company has the lowest number of customer complaints of all airlines by a factor of three.

When employees join a new company and enter a new corporate culture, they typically go through three stages of assimilation. When hired, they become *aware of the organization's values* without sharing them personally. In the second stage, these beliefs start to have more meaning and the employee *uses them as a guide* for appropriate behavior at work. Real efficiencies are gained in the final stage, when the employee moves from simple compliance to *internalization* and comes to hold corporate values as personal beliefs. In this last phase, employees become driven by intrinsic rewards—deriving personal satisfaction from acting in a matter that is congruent with the firm's beliefs and values.

A corporate culture is manifested through artifacts, shared values, and basic assumptions. *Artifacts* are visible or audible processes, policies, and procedures that support an important cultural belief. One such artifact is a company's dress code. IBM has a dress code that stipulates proper business attire. Lotus, by contrast, reflects its more relaxed culture by permitting T-shirts and sandals.[16] *Shared values* explain why things should be as they are. Shared values often reinforce areas of competitive advantage and can be found in internal corporate language. The words can be well defined within mission statements and codes of ethics or ambiguously embedded within company lingo. Either way, these words and phrases are used to define the image a firm wants to portray. Microsoft, for example, supports a culture of high energy, drive, intellect, and entrepreneurship. The day-to-day company language is filled with "nerdisms" such as *supercool* and *totally random*. Employees touted as having high bandwidth (energetic and creative thinkers) are the most respected.[17] Finally, *basic assumptions* are invisible reasons why group members perceive, think, and feel the way they do about operational issues. They are sometimes demonstrated in corporate myths and stories that highlight corporate values. These legends are of considerable value because employees can identify with them and easily share them with others.

A pronounced corporate culture can be an advantage or an impediment in times of rapid change. On the one hand, the continuance of core values can help employees become comfortable with or adjust to new challenges or practices. On the other hand, a company's prevailing organizational culture can inhibit or defeat a change effort when the consequences of the change are feared. For example, in a company in which consensus decision-making is the norm, a change to more top-down decision-making is likely to be resisted. Similarly, an organization focused on quarterly results will culturally resist a shift to a longer-term time horizon. These reactions do not constitute overt resistance to change. Rather, they represent to-be-expected responses fostered by the cultural elements ingrained over a long period of time in the organization. The failure to recognize and work within the prevailing cultural elements can doom a change agenda. For example, a large global pharmaceutical company discovered that R&D professionals resisted their promotions to management. An examination revealed that the resistance stemmed from an organizational culture bias that prevented them from competing with their peers for career rewards.[18]

STRATEGIC RESOURCES AND COMPETITIVE ADVANTAGE

Strategic thinking focuses on developing and maintaining competitive advantages for an organization. A firm has a *competitive advantage* when it is successful in designing and implementing a value-creating strategy that competitors are not currently using. That competitive advantage is sustainable when current or new competitors are not able to copy or supplant it.

A competitive advantage is often created by combining multiple strengths. Firms look for ways to exploit competencies and advantages at different points in the value chain to add value in different ways. Southwest Airlines' 15-minute turnaround time, for example, enjoys a competitive advantage that saves the firm $175 million annually in capital expenditures, and differentiates the firm by allowing it to offer more flights per plane per day. Use of value analysis helps a firm to focus on areas in which it enjoys competitive advantages, and to outsource functions in which it does not.

To enhance its cost leadership position, Taco Bell outsources many food-preparation functions, thereby allowing it to cut prices, reduce employees, and free up 40% of its kitchen space.

It is important for executives to understand the nature and sources of a firm's competitive advantages. They should also make sure that middle managers understand the competitive advantages because the managers' awareness of them allows for a more effective exploitation of such advantages and leads to increased firm performance. Building a competitive advantage is therefore rooted in identifying, practicing, strengthening, and instilling throughout the organization those leadership traits that improve the firm's reputation among its stakeholders. As a consequence, a focus on organizational learning and on creating, retaining, and motivating a skilled and knowledgeable work force may be the best way for executives to foster competitive advantages in a rapidly changing business environment.

Value Chain Analysis

In competitive terms, *value* is the amount a buyer is willing to pay for what a firm provides. Customers derive value from product differentiation, product cost, and the ability of the firm to meet their needs. Value-creating activities are therefore the discrete building blocks of competitive advantage.

A *value chain* is a model of a business process. It depicts the value-creation process as a series of activities, beginning with processing raw materials and ending with sales and service to end users. *Value chain analysis* involves the study of costs and elements of product or service differentiation throughout the chain of activities and linkages to determine present and potential sources of competitive advantage.

The value chain divides a firm's business process into component activities that add value: primary activities that contribute to the physical creation of the product, and support activities that assist the primary activities and each other, as shown in Figure 3-3.

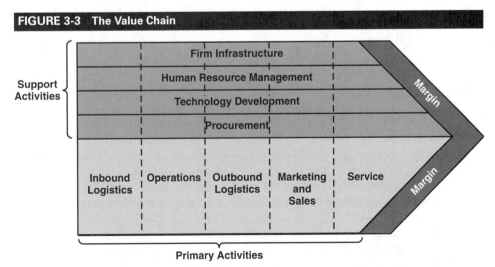

FIGURE 3-3 The Value Chain

Source: Reprinted by permission of *Harvard Business Review.* The Value Chain. "How Information Gives You Competitive Advantage; the Information Revolution is Transforming the Nature of Competition," by M. E. Porter and V. E. Millar, 63(4) 1985. Copyright © 1985 by the Harvard Business School Publishing Corporation; all rights reserved.

Charles Schwab successfully utilized its expertise in a support activity to create value in a primary activity. The firm offers a broad range of distribution channels (primary activity) for its brokerage services and holds extensive expertise in information technology (IT) and brokerage systems (support activities). Schwab uses its IT knowledge to create two new distribution channels for brokerage services—E-Schwab on the Internet and the Telebroker touch-tone telephone-brokering service—both of which provide value by delivering low-cost services that competitors could not provide.[19]

Once a firm's primary, support, and activity types are defined, value chain analysis assigns operating costs and assets to all value-creating activities. Activity-based cost accounting is often used to determine whether a competitive advantage exists.

A firm *differentiates* itself from its competitors when it provides something unique that is valuable to buyers beyond a low price. Dell Computer Corporation's ability to sell, build-to-order, and ship a computer to the customer within a few days is a unique differentiator of its value chain. Benetton, the Italian casual wear company, reconfigured its traditional outsourced manufacturing and distribution network.[20] Its executives reasoned that the company could remain flexible and achieve a high level of performance with a more complex network architecture in which it directly oversees key business processes throughout the supply chain. If specific activities reduce a buyer's cost or provide a higher level of buyer satisfaction, customers might be willing to pay a premium price. Sources of differentiation of primary activities that provide a higher level of buyer satisfaction include build-to-order manufacturing, efficient and on-time delivery of goods, promptness in responding to customer service requests, and high quality.

It is important to identify the value that individual primary and support activities contribute beyond their costs. Different segments of the value chain represent potential sources of profit and therefore define *profit pools*.[21] Value chain analysis showed Nike and Reebok how their core competencies in product design (a support activity) and marketing and sales (primary activities) created value for customers and led them to outsource almost all other activities.[22] In a second case, after completing a detailed value chain analysis, Millennium Pharmaceuticals opted to shift from drug research in the upstream portion of the industry to drug manufacturing downstream, to improve its profitability. This strategy was derived from the firm's clearer understanding of the entire pharmaceutical value chain and its newly recognized ability to better exploit different profit pools.[23]

Analyzing the value chains of competitors, customers, and suppliers can help a firm add value by focusing on the needs of downstream customers or the weaknesses of upstream suppliers.[24] Dow Chemical captures value from downstream rubber glove producers, to whom it used to sell chemicals, by making the gloves itself. BASF adds value by leveraging its core competencies in the paint-coating process by painting car doors for auto manufacturers, instead of just selling them the paint.

Value chain analysis can also be used to shape responses to changing upstream and downstream market conditions through collaboration with customers and suppliers to improve speed, cut costs, and enhance the end customer's perception of value. This is especially true as intercompany links such as electronic data integration systems, strategic alliances, just-in-time manufacturing, electronic markets, and networked companies blur the boundaries of today's organizations.

Approaching value chain analysis as a shared process involving the different members of the chain can optimize a firm's value creation by minimizing collective costs. Dell, for example, shares information about its customers with its suppliers. This improves its suppliers' ability to forecast demand, which results in reduced inventory and logistics costs for itself and its suppliers. Home Depot and General Electric established an alliance between their value chains that reduces direct and indirect costs for each firm. A Web-based application links Home Depot's point-of-purchase data to GE's e-business system and enables Home Depot to ship directly to customers from GE. The value chain to value chain connection enables Home Depot to sell more GE products and reduce the inventory in its warehouses. In addition, GE can use the real-time demand information from Home Depot to adjust the production rate of appliances.

With advances in information technology and the Internet, companies can monitor value creation across many activities and linkages. For purposes of monitoring, it is useful to distinguish between the physical and virtual components of the value chain. The *physical value chain* represents the use of raw materials and labor to deliver a tangible product. The *virtual value chain* represents the information flows underlying the physical activities evident within a firm. Engineering teams at Ford Motor Company optimize the physical design process of a vehicle using real-time collaboration in a virtual workplace. Oracle Corporation is a front-runner in adding virtual value for the customer by using the Internet to directly test and distribute its software products.[25]

ANALYZING INTERNAL CHANGE FORCES

In Chapter 2, we focused on change forces that emanate from a company's external strategic environment. A second set of drivers for strategic change comes from within the organization or from its immediate stakeholders. Disappointing financial performance, new owners or executives, limitations on growth with current strategies, scarcity of critical resources, and internal cultural changes are examples of conditions that give rise to pressures for change.

Because internal resistance forces can reduce a company's capacity to adapt and chart a new course, they deserve a strategist's careful attention. Organizational resistance to change can take four basic forms: (1) structural, organizational rigidities, (2) closed mind-sets reflecting obsolete business beliefs and strategies, (3) entrenched cultures reflecting values, behaviors, and skills that are not conducive to change, and (4) counterproductive momentum that is not in tune with current strategic requirements.[26]

The four forms of resistance represent very different strategic challenges. Internal structures and systems, including technology, can be changed relatively quickly in most companies. Converting closed minds to the need for change, or changing a corporate culture, is considerably harder. Counterproductive change is especially difficult to remedy because it typically involves altering all three forms of resistance—structures and systems have to be rethought, mind-sets must change, and new behaviors and skills have to be learned.

The Company Life Cycle

The forms and strengths of organizational resistance forces that are likely to develop greatly depend on a company's history, performance, and culture. Nevertheless, some patterns can be anticipated. Companies go through life cycles. A cycle begins when a founder or founding team organizes a start-up. At this time, a vision or purpose is established, the initial direction for the company is set, and the necessary resources are marshaled to transform this vision into reality. In these early stages, the identities of the founders and that of the company are difficult to separate.

As companies grow, more-formal systems are needed to handle a variety of functions. The transition from informality to a more-formal organizational structure can stimulate or hinder strategic change. This passage to organizational maturity, often described as the *entrepreneurial-managerial transition,* poses a dilemma familiar to many companies: how to maintain an entrepreneurial spirit while moving toward an organizational structure increasingly focused on control. Some companies—Lotus Development Corporation and Microsoft, for example—have made this transition with relative ease, while others continue to struggle.

Growth makes organizational learning a requirement for continued success. The evolution of management processes, such as delegation of authority, coordination of effort, and collaboration among organizational units, can have an increasing influence on a company's effectiveness in responding to environmental and internal challenges. In younger companies, the internal operating environment is frequently characterized by greater ambiguity than in established organizations. Often the ambiguity that encouraged entrepreneurship and innovation leads to a lack of control in a rapidly growing company and can cause the firm to lose its strategic focus.

Evolving and established companies share the pervasive challenge of finding strategies to manage growth. For many evolving companies, uncontrolled growth is a major concern. As they try to cope with rapid growth, they find that success can mask a host of organizational development problems. Dilemmas of leadership can develop, loss of focus becomes an issue, communication becomes harder, skill development falls behind, and stress becomes evident. In established companies, the pressure to continue to grow faster can skew strategic thinking. Ill-considered acquisitions or market expansions; forays into new, untested technologies; deviations from developing core skills; and frequent exhortations for more entrepreneurial thinking are indicative of the challenges experienced in more mature companies.

Stakeholder Analysis

In assessing a company's strategic position, it is important to identify key stakeholders inside and outside the organization, the roles they play in fulfilling the organization's mission, and the values they bring to the process. As we saw in Chapter 2, external stakeholders—key customers, suppliers, alliance partners, and regulatory agencies—have a major influence on a firm's strategic options. A firm's internal stakeholders—its owners, board of directors, CEO, executives, managers, and employees—are equally important.

In determining the company's objectives and strategies, executives must recognize the legitimate rights of the firm's stakeholders. Each of these interested parties has justifiable reasons for expecting—and often for demanding—that the company will satisfy its claim. In general, stockholders claim competitive returns on their investment, employees seek job satisfaction, customers want what they pay for, suppliers seek dependable buyers, governments want adherence to legislation, unions seek member benefits, competitors want fair competition, local communities want the firm to be a responsible citizen, and the general public expects the firm's existence to improve their nation's quality of life.

The general claims of stakeholders are reflected in thousands of specific demands on every firm — high wages, pure air, job security, product quality, community service, taxes, occupational health and safety regulations, equal employment opportunity regulations, product variety, wide markets, career opportunities, company growth, investment security, high ROI, and many, many more. Although most, perhaps all, of these claims represent desirable ends, they cannot be pursued with equal emphasis. They must be assigned priorities in accordance with the relative emphasis that the firm will give them. That emphasis is a consequence of the criteria that the firm uses in its strategic decision-making.

The Balanced Scorecard

The Balanced Scorecard is a set of measures designed to provide strategists with a quick, yet comprehensive, view of the business.[27] Developed by Robert Kaplan and David Norton, the Scorecard asks managers to look at their business from customer, company capability, innovation and learning, and financial perspectives. It provides answers to four basic questions: (1) How do customers see us? (2) At what must we excel? (3) Can we continue to improve and create value? (4) How do we look to our company's shareholders?

The Balanced Scorecard requires managers to translate a broad *customer-driven* mission statement into factors that directly relate to customer concerns such as product quality, on-time delivery, product performance, service, and cost. Measures are defined for each factor based on customers' perspectives and expectations, and objectives for each measure are articulated and translated into specific performance metrics. Apple Computer Corporation uses the Balanced Scorecard to introduce customer satisfaction metrics. Historically, Apple was a technology and product-focused company that competed by designing better computers. Getting employees to focus on customer satisfaction metrics enables Apple to function now as a customer-driven company.

Customer-based measures are important, but they must be translated into measures of what the company must do *internally* to meet its customers' expectations. Once these measures are translated into operational objectives such as cycle time, product quality, productivity, and cost, managers must focus on the internal business processes that enable the organization to meet the customer's needs.

Customer-based and internal business process measures directly relate to competitive success. The ability to create new products, provide value to customers, and improve operating efficiencies provides the basis for entering new markets that drive incremental revenue, margins, and shareholder value. Financial performance measures signal whether the company's strategy and its implementation are achieving the company objectives that relate to profitability, growth, and shareholder value. Measures such as cash flow, sales growth, operating income, market share, return on assets, return on investment, return on equity, and stock price quantify the financial effects of strategies and link them to other elements of the Balanced Scorecard. A failure to convert improved operational performance, as measured in the Scorecard, into improved financial performance should spur executives to rethink the company's strategy.

The application of the Balanced Scorecard has evolved into an overall management system. In essence, the Scorecard encompasses four management processes—translating a vision, communicating goals and linking rewards to performance, improving business planning, and gathering feedback and learning. Separately, and in combination, the processes contribute to linking long-term strategic objectives with short-term actions.[28]

The objective of *translating a vision* is to clarify and gain employee support for that vision. For people to be able to act effectively on a vision statement, that statement must be expressed in terms of an integrated set of objectives and measures, based on recognized long-term drivers of success. The application of the Scorecard is also useful in highlighting gaps in employee skill sets, information technology, and processes that can hamper an organization's ability to execute a given strategy.

Thorough and broad-based *communication* is essential to ensure that employees understand the firm's objectives and the strategies that are designed to achieve them. Business unit and individual goals must then be aligned with those of the company to create ownership and accountability. *Linking rewards* to the Balanced Scorecard is a direct means of measuring and rewarding contributions to strategic performance. Clearly defined, objective performance measures and incentives are key to creating the right motivational environment.

Creating a Balanced Scorecard forces companies to *integrate* their strategic planning and budgeting processes. The output of the business-planning process consists of a set of long-term targets in all four areas of the scorecard (customer, internal, innovation/learning, and financial), a set of clearly defined initiatives to meet the targets, an agreed-upon allocation of resources to support these initiatives, and a set of appropriate measures to monitor progress. In this process, financial budgeting remains important but does not drive or overshadow the other elements.

Finally, managers must constantly gather *feedback* on the Balanced Scorecard's short-term measurements to monitor progress in achieving the long-term strategy and to *learn* how performance can be improved. Deviations from expected outcomes indicate that assumptions regarding market conditions, competitive pressures, and internal capabilities need to be revisited. As such, this feedback assists in assessing whether a chosen strategy needs to be revised in light of updated information about competitive conditions.

Strengths, Weaknesses, Opportunities, and Threats

SWOT analysis—the sizing up of a company's strengths, weaknesses, external opportunities, and threats—is a helpful tool for generating a list of factors for strategic consideration. *Strengths and weaknesses* relate to internal factors. They can include skills, expertise or technological know-how, organizational resources, competitive capabilities, and positional advantages or disadvantages defined by such variables as market share, brand recognition, or distribution capabilities, alliances, and other partnering arrangements. *Opportunities and threats* stem from a company's external competitive environment. The exit of a competitor, for example, spells opportunity. New regulations or the emergence of lower-cost technologies, on the other hand, poses threats. Figure 3-4 documents examples of issues to consider when evaluating a company's strengths, weaknesses, opportunities, and threats.

SWOT analysis can be helpful to an overall assessment of a company's competitive position. Simply classifying variables under different SWOT headings has little value,

Potential Internal Strengths	*Potential Internal Weaknesses*
• Core competencies in key areas	• No clear strategic direction
• Adequate financial resources	• Obsolete facilities
• Well-thought-of by buyers	• Subpar profitability because . . .
• An acknowledged market leader	• Lack of managerial depth and talent
• Well-conceived functional area strategies	• Missing some key skills or competencies
• Access to economies of scale	• Poor track record in implementing strategy
• Insulated (at least somewhat) from strong competitive pressures	• Plagued with internal operating problems
• Proprietary technology	• Falling behind in R&D
• Cost advantages	• Too narrow a product line
• Better advertising campaigns	• Weak market image
• Product innovation skills	• Weak distribution network
• Proven management	• Below-average marketing skills
• Ahead on experience curve	• Unable to finance needed changes in strategy
• Better manufacturing capability	• Higher overall unit costs relative to key competitors
• Superior technological skills	• Other?
• Other?	

Potential External Opportunities	*Potential External Threats*
• Ability to serve additional customer groups or expand into new markets or segments	• Entry of lower-cost foreign competitors
• Ways to expand product line to meet broader range of customer needs	• Rising sales of substitute products
	• Slower market growth
• Ability to transfer skills or technological know-how to new products or businesses	• Adverse shifts in foreign exchange rates and trade policies of foreign governments
• Integrating forward or backward	• Costly regulatory requirements
• Falling trade barriers in attractive foreign markets	• Vulnerability to recession and business cycle
• Complacency among rival firms	• Growing bargaining power of customers or suppliers
• Ability to grow rapidly because of strong increases in market demand	• Changing buyer needs and tastes
• Emerging new technologies	• Adverse demographic changes
	• Other?

FIGURE 3-4   SWOT Analysis

Source: From Arthur A. Thompson Jr. and A. J. Strickland III, *Strategic Management,* 11th edition, 2002. Reprinted by permission of McGraw-Hill Company, Inc., New York, NY.

and suggests nothing about strategic options or their viability. However, the identification of high-impact variables invites meaningful discussions. For example, in trying to answer the question "How secure is the firm's current competitive position?" it is useful to ask such SWOT-related questions as "Will the company's competitive position become stronger or weaker if the present strategy is continued?"

NOTES

1. V. A. Rice, "Why EVA works for Variety," *Chief Executive,* 1996, 110: pp. 40–44.
2. K. Lehn and A. K. Makhija, "EVA & MVA: As Performance Measures and Signals for Strategic Change," *Strategy & Leadership,* 1996, 24 (3): pp. 34–41.
3. S. Tully, "The EVA Advantage," *Fortune,* 1999, 139 (6): p. 210.
4. J. B. White, "Value-Based Pay Systems Are Gaining Popularity," *The Wall Street Journal,* April 10, 1997, p. B8.
5. J. L. Dodd and J. Johns, "EVA Reconsidered," *Business and Economic Review,* 1999, 45 (3): pp. 13–18.
6. R. Oliver, "The Return on Human Capital," *Journal of Business Strategy,* July/August 2001, pp. 7–10.
7. J. Byrne, A. Reinhardt, and R. D. Hof, "The Search for the Young and Gifted: Why Talent Counts," *Business Week,* October 4, 1999.
8. J. S. Brown and P. Duguid, "Balancing Act: How to Capture Knowledge Without Killing It," *Harvard Business Review,* 2000, 78: pp. 73–80.
9. R. Cross and L. Baird, "Technology Is Not Enough: Improving Performance by Building Organizational Memory," *Sloan Management Review,* 2000, 41: pp. 69–78.
10. A. K. Gupta and V. Govindarajan, "Knowledge Management's Social Dimension: Lessons from Nucor Steel," *Sloan Management Review,* 2000, 42: pp. 71–83.
11. J. B. Quinn, "Strategic Outsourcing: Leveraging Knowledge Capabilities," *Sloan Management Review,* 1999, 40 (4): pp. 9–22.
12. C. K. Prahalad and G. Hamel, "The Core Competence of the Corporation," *Harvard Business Review,* (May–June 1990): pp. 79–93.
13. L. Soupata, "Managing Culture for Competitive Advantage at United Parcel Service," *Journal of Organizational Excellence,* 2001, 20 (3): pp. 19–26.
14. D. W. Young, "The Six Levers for Managing Organizational Culture," *Business Horizons,* 2000, 43 (5): pp. 19–34.
15. D. Harville, "Hidden Value: How Great Companies Achieve Extraordinary Results with Ordinary People," *Personnel Psychology,* 2001, 54: pp. 746–750.
16. Young, "The Six Levers for Managing Organizational Culture."
17. K. Rebello and E. I. Schwartz, "Microsoft: Bill Gates's Baby Is on Top of the World. Can it Stay There?" *Business Week,* April 19, 1999.
18. J. R. Ross, "Does Corporate Culture Contribute to Performance?" *American International College Journal of Business,* Spring 2000: pp. 4–9.
19. J. Webb and C. Gile, "Reversing the Value Chain," *The Journal of Business Strategy,* 2001, 22 (2): pp. 13–17.
20. A. Camuffo, P. Romano, and A. Vinelli, "Back to the Future: Benetton Transforms Its Global Network," *Sloan Management Review,* 2001, 43: pp. 46–52.
21. O. Gadiesh and J. L. Gilbert, "Profit Pools: A Fresh Look At Strategy," *Harvard Business Review,* 1998, 76 (3): pp. 139–147.
22. J. H. Sheridan, "Managing the Chain," *Industry Week,* September 6, 1999, 248 (16): pp. 50–55.
23. D. Champion, "Mastering the Value Chain," *Harvard Business Review,* 2001, 79 (6): pp. 109–115.
24. F. Budde, B. R. Elliott, G. Farha, C. R. Palmer, and R. Steffen, "The Chemistry of Knowledge," *The McKinsey Quarterly,* 2000, (4): pp. 98–107.
25. J. F. Rayport and J. J. Sviokla, "Exploiting the Virtual Value Chain," *Harvard Business Review,* 1995, 73 (6): pp. 75–85.
26. P. Strebel, "Choosing the Right Change Path," *California Management Review,* 1994, 36: p. 30.
27. R. Kaplan and D. P. Norton, "Building a Strategy Focused Organization," *Ivey Business Journal,* May–June 2001, pp. 12–17.
28. R. Kaplan and D. P. Norton, "Leading Change with the Balanced Scorecard," *Financial Executive,* September 2001, pp. 64–66.

Formulating Business Unit Strategy

INTRODUCTION

Business unit strategy involves creating a profitable competitive position for a business within a specific industry or market segment. Sometimes called competitive strategy, its principal focus is on *how* a firm should compete in a given competitive setting. In contrast, corporate strategy, the subject of Chapters 6 and 7, is concerned with the identification of market arenas *where* a corporation can compete successfully and *how,* as a parent company, it can add value to its strategic business units (SBUs).

Deciding how to compete in a specific market is a complex issue. Optimal strategies depend on many factors including *the nature of the industry, the company's mission, goals and objectives, its current position and core competencies,* and *major competitors' strategic choices.*

We begin our discussion by examining the *logic* behind strategic thinking at the business unit level. In this section, we address the basic question: What determines profitability at the business unit level? We look at the relative importance of the industry in which a company competes, and of its competitive position within the industry, and we identify the drivers that determine sustainable competitive advantage. This logic naturally suggests a number of *generic strategy choices*—broad strategy prescriptions that define the principal dimensions of competition at the business unit level. The generic strategy that is most attractive and the form that it should take vary considerably with the specific opportunities and challenges. The chapter next deals with the question of how to assess a strategic challenge. The chapter then introduces a variety of useful techniques for generating and evaluating strategic alternatives, including *growth vector analysis, profit pool analysis, gap analysis, competitor analysis,* and *product life cycle analysis.* The final section addresses the issue of designing a profitable business model.

FOUNDATIONS

Strategic Logic at the Business Unit Level

What are the principal factors behind a business unit's profitability? How important are product superiority, cost, marketing and distribution effectiveness, and other factors? How important is the nature of the industry?

Though there are no simple answers to such questions, and the attractiveness of different strategic options varies greatly with the competitive situation analyzed, much has been learned about what drives competitive success at the business unit level. Professor Michael Porter has articulated a *strategic logic,* depicted in Figure 4-1, which guides much of our strategic thinking at the business level.[1]

This logic begins with the observation that, at the broadest level, firm success is explained by two principal factors: the *attractiveness of the industry* in which a firm competes and its *relative position* within that industry. For example, the seemingly insatiable demand for new products in the early history of the software industry guaranteed big profits for the industry leaders and for many of their smaller rivals. In the fiercely competitive beer industry, on the other hand, relative positioning is a far more important determinant of profitability, as Budweiser's unprecedented performance has shown.

How Much Does Industry Matter?

In a comprehensive study of business performance in 4-digit SIC industry categories, McGahan and Porter provided an answer to the question: How much does industry matter? They found that industry, segment, and corporate parent accounted for 32 percent, 4 percent, and 19 percent, respectively, of the aggregate variance in business profits. These results support the conclusion that industry characteristics are an important determinant

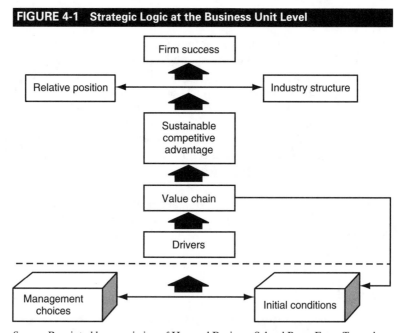

FIGURE 4-1 Strategic Logic at the Business Unit Level

Source: Reprinted by permission of Harvard Business School Press. From *Toward a Dynamic Theory of Strategy* by Michael E. Porter et al. Boston, MA 1994, p. 432. Copyright © 1994 by the Harvard Business School Publishing Corporation; all rights reserved.

of profit potential. Industry directly accounted for 36 percent of the explained total variation in profitability.[2]

Relative Position

The relative profitability of rival firms depends on the *nature of their competitive position,* i.e., on their ability to create a *sustainable competitive advantage* vis-a-vis their competitors. Porter identifies two generic forms of sustainable competitive positioning: a competitive advantage based on *lower delivered cost* and one based on the ability to *differentiate* products or services from those of competitors and command a price premium relative to the cost incurred.[3]

Whether lowest cost or differentiation is most effective depends, among other factors, on a firm's choice of *competitive scope.* The scope of a competitive strategy includes such elements as the number of product and buyer segments served, the number of different geographic locations in which the firm competes, the extent to which it is vertically integrated, and the degree to which it must coordinate its positioning with related businesses in which the firm is invested.

Decisions about scope and how to create a competitive advantage are made on the basis of a detailed understanding of what customers value and what capabilities and opportunities a company has relative to its competitors. In this sense, strategy reflects a firm's configuration and how the different elements interrelate. Competitive advantage results when a company has a better understanding of what customers desire and when it learns to meet those customer needs at a lower cost than rivals, or when it creates buyer value in unique ways that allow it to charge a premium.

How Important Is Market Share?

The relative importance of market share as a strategic goal at the business unit level has been the subject of considerable controversy. Arguing that profitability should be the primary goal of strategy, Adrian Slywotzky and David Morrison believe executives have been led astray by the principal pursuit of market share.[4] Many failed companies have achieved high market shares, including A&P in grocery sales, Intel in memory products, and WordPerfect in word processors. Thus, executives must ask themselves: Am I managing for volume growth or value growth?[5]

Although no manager should pursue growth for growth's sake, there is evidence that market share is an important determinant of long-term profitability. Bradley Gale and Robert Buzzell, in reviewing the evidence on this subject, put it succinctly: "Large market share is both a reward for providing better value and a means of realizing lower costs. Under most circumstances, enterprises that have achieved a large share of the markets they serve are considerably more profitable than their smaller-share rivals. This connection between market share and profitability has been recognized by corporate executives and consultants . . . ."[6]

Findings From the PIMS Project

The Marketing Science Institute at the Harvard Business School undertook research into the relative profitability of different market strategies. This PIMS (Profit Impact of Market Strategy) project involved more than 600 businesses over a period of more than 15 years.[7]

The major findings of the PIMS study are:

1. Absolute and relative market share are strongly correlated with return on investment (ROI). Businesses with higher market shares were generally more profitable because of economies of scale, experience effects, market power, and the quality of management.
2. Product quality is key to market leadership and allows companies with larger market shares to charge higher prices and therefore achieve higher margins.
3. ROI is positively correlated with market growth.
4. Vertical integration can be beneficial later in the product life cycle. Partial vertical integration should be avoided. Forward integration is more profitable than backward integration.
5. High investment intensity tends to depress ROI, as do high inventory levels.
6. Capacity utilization is critical for businesses with a high level of capital intensity; companies with small market shares are particularly vulnerable.

The PIMS findings help to explain many business success stories through the 1980s. However, they also help to explain many business performance declines of the 1990s and the early 2000s. The current dynamic, technology-driven experiences of the past decade bear little resemblance to the marketplace where successful competitors followed the PIMS model. Thus, although the lessons from the PIMS research were beneficial at the time that they were first taught, the number of business settings in which they have enduring relevance is decreasing rapidly.

PORTER'S GENERIC STRATEGIES

Differentiation or Low Cost?

Earlier, we distinguished between two *generic* competitive strategic postures: *low cost* and *differentiation*. They are called generic because in principle they apply to any business and any industry. However, the relative attractiveness of different generic strategies is related to choices about competitive scope. If a company chooses a relatively broad target market—Wal-Mart, for example—a low-cost strategy is aimed at *cost leadership*. Such a strategy aggressively exploits opportunities for cost reduction through economies of scale and cumulative learning (experience effects) in purchasing and manufacturing, and generally calls for proportionately low expenditures on R&D, marketing, and overhead. Cost leaders generally charge less for their products and services than rivals, and aim for a significant share of the market by appealing primarily to budget-sensitive customers. Their low prices serve as an entry barrier to potential competitors. As long as they maintain their relative cost advantage, cost leaders can maintain a defensible position in the marketplace.

With a more-narrow scope, a low-cost strategy is based on *cost focus*. As with any focus strategy, a small, well-defined market niche—a particular group of customers or geographic region—is selected to the exclusion of others. Then, in the case of cost focus, only activities directly relevant to serving that niche are undertaken, at the lowest possible cost.

Southwest Airlines is renowned for its cost focus strategy. A low-fare carrier that in 2000 had the highest profit margins in the airline industry, Southwest Airlines grew

4,048 percent between 1990 and 1999. In 2000, the company had $4.2 billion in total operating revenue and $625.2 million in profits. Its low-cost, no-frills strategy has been highly successful in the U.S. domestic market.[8]

The cost focus strategy is based on a narrow scope, with a small, well-defined market niche. Southwest concentrates on short-haul routes with high traffic densities, and offers frequent flights throughout the day. Efficiency has been improved by eliminating costs associated with hub routes involving large major U.S. airports. Operating in only 57 cities in 28 states, Southwest targets secondary airports because of their lower cost structures.

Southwest's fundamentally different operating structure allows it to charge lower fares than more established airlines. A typical flight, which lasts one hour on average, has no assigned seats; in-flight service consists of drinks and snacks only, and the company does not offer transfer of luggage to other airlines.

Southwest's fleet consists of 284 Boeing 737s, which make more than 2,400 flights per day. Having one type of aircraft allows for greater efficiency and easier turnarounds. All Southwest 737s use the same equipment, thereby keeping training and maintenance costs down. Finally, high asset utilization, reflected in a turnaround time averaging twenty minutes, which is less than half the industry average, reduces its operating expenses by 25 percent.

Differentiation postures can similarly be tied to decisions of scope. A *differentiation* strategy aimed at a broad, mass market seeks to create uniqueness on an industry-wide basis. Walt Disney Productions and Nike are examples. Broad-scale differentiation can be achieved through product design, brand image, technology, distribution, service, or a combination of these elements. Finally, like cost focus, a *differentiated focus* strategy is aimed at a well-defined segment of the market and targets customers willing to pay for value added, as depicted in Figure 4-2.

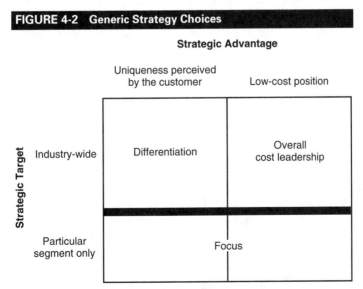

FIGURE 4-2   Generic Strategy Choices

Source: Reprinted with the permission of The Free Press, an imprint of Simon & Schuster Adult Publishing Group, from *Competitive Strategy: Techniques for Analyzing Industries and Competitors* by Michael E. Porter. Copyright © 1980, 1998 by The Free Press.

Requirements for Success

The two generic routes—*low cost* and *differentiation*—are fundamentally different. Achieving *cost leadership* requires a ruthless devotion to minimizing costs through continuous improvement in manufacturing, process engineering, and other cost-reducing strategies. Scale and scope effects must be leveraged in all aspects of the value-creation process—in the design of products and services, purchasing practices, and distribution. In addition, organizationally, achieving and sustaining cost leadership requires tight control and an organizational structure and incentive system supportive of a cost-focused discipline.

Differentiation requires an altogether different approach. Here, the concern is for value added. Differentiation has multiple objectives. The primary objective is to redefine the rules by which customers arrive at their purchase decisions by offering something unique that is valuable. In doing so, companies also seek to erect barriers to imitation. Differentiation strategies are often misunderstood; spray painting the product green is *not* differentiation. Differentiation is a strategic choice to provide something of value to the customer other than a low price. One way to differentiate a product or service is to add functionality. There are, however, many other, sometimes more-effective ways to differentiate. R&D aimed at enhancing product quality and durability (Maytag) is a viable element of a differentiation strategy. Investing in brand equity (Coca-Cola) and pioneering new ways of distribution (Avon Cosmetics) are others.

There is considerable evidence that the most successful differentiation strategies involve multiple sources of differentiation. Higher-quality raw materials, unique product design, more reliable manufacture, superior marketing and distribution programs, and quicker service all contribute to set a company's offering apart from rival products. The use of more than one source of differentiation makes it harder for competitors to effectively imitate. In addition to using multiple sources, integrating the different dimensions of value added—functionality, and economic and psychological value—is key. Effective differentiation thus requires explicit decisions about how much value to add, where to add such value, and how to communicate such added value to the customer. Critically for the firm, customers must be willing to pay a premium relative to the cost of achieving the differentiation. Successful differentiation therefore requires a thorough understanding of what customers value, what relative importance they attach to the satisfaction of different needs and wants, and how much they are willing to pay.

Risks

Each generic posture carries its own unique risks. Cost leaders must concern themselves with technological change that can nullify past investments in scale economics or accumulated learning. In an increasingly global economy, firms that rely on cost leadership are particularly vulnerable to new entrants from other parts of the world that can take advantage of lower factor costs. The biggest challenge to differentiators is *imitation.* Imitation narrows actual and perceived differentiation. If this occurs, buyers might change their minds about what constitutes differentiation, and then change their loyalties and preferences.

The goal of each strategic generic posture is to create sustainability. For cost leaders, sustainability requires continually improving efficiency, looking for less expensive sources of supply, and seeking ways to reduce manufacturing and distribution costs.

For differentiators, sustainability requires firms to erect barriers to entry around their dimensions of uniqueness, to use multiple sources of differentiation, and to create switching costs for customers. Organizationally, a differentiation strategy calls for strong coordination among R&D, product development and marketing, and incentives aimed at value creation and creativity.

A Success Story: Dell Computer

The story of Dell Computer's rise in the PC industry illustrates how a relentless pursuit of cost leadership and a close alignment between strategy and business design can pay off. Michael Dell, the company's founder and a consummate entrepreneur, defied critics who predicted that his mail-order model would not work.

Convinced he had a winning formula for selling personal computers, Dell turned a low-margin mail-order operation into a high-profit, high-service business by challenging every aspect of PC selling and manufacturing. The company successfully applied its just-in-time manufacturing philosophy to the rest of its supply chain—requiring, for example, that critical components be warehoused within 15 minutes' travel time of a Dell factory. In addition, by marrying this low-cost, speed-based business model to the new principles of electronic commerce, Dell created a sustainable competitive advantage.

In relatively short order, Dell moved from a challenger to the number-one seller of PCs over the Web. Many corporations that were willing to buy over the telephone preferred electronic purchasing. Consequently, Dell stock became one of the best high-technology growth investments and its business model the envy of the industry. According to *Business Week,* Dell converts an average sale into cash in less than twenty-four hours, by emphasizing credit cards and electronic payment. In contrast, industry giant Compaq Computer Corp., which sells primarily through dealers, takes 35 days, and even mail-order rival Gateway takes more than 16 days.

Competitors are working hard to catch up. IBM, Compaq, and Hewlett-Packard are trying to cut production time and improve service. IBM, for example, decided to allow dealers to assemble PCs for its business customers. Compaq is designing its own Internet connection, allowing customers to manage everything from ordering a machine to scheduling software updates online. However, imitation strategies have limitations, especially when the underlying business model is hard to change. Consider production, for example. Although machines from Compaq and IBM can sit on dealer shelves for months, Dell does not order components until an order is booked. With rapidly falling prices, that can translate into a significant profit advantage in components alone.

Critique of Porter's Generic Strategies

The majority of research studies on the efficacy of Porter's framework indicate that generic strategies are not always viable. Low-cost strategies are less effective when low cost is the industry norm. Further, there is evidence that executives reject Porter's generic strategies in favor of strategies that combine elements of cost leadership, differentiation, and flexibility to meet customer needs.[9]

The most common arguments against Porter's generic strategies are that low-cost production and differentiation are not mutually exclusive and that when they can exist together in a firm's strategy, they result in sustained profitability.[10] The preconditions for a cost leadership strategy stem from the industry's structure, whereas the preconditions for differentiation stem from customer tastes. Because these two factors are independent, the opportunity of a firm's pursuing both cost leadership and differentiation strategies should always be considered.

In fact, differentiation can permit a firm to attain a low-cost position.[11] For example, expenditures to differentiate a product affect demand by creating loyalty, which decreases the price elasticity for the product. It also broadens product appeal, enabling the firm to increase market share at a given price, and it increases volume sold. Differentiation initially increases unit cost. However, the firm can reduce unit cost in the long run if costs fall due to learning economies, economies of scale, and economies of scope. Conversely, the savings generated from low-cost production permit a firm to increase spending on marketing, service, and product enhancement, thereby producing differentiation.[12]

Finally, the possibility of providing both improved quality and lower costs exists within the total quality management framework. High quality and high productivity are complementary; and low quality is associated with higher costs.[13]

There are also dangers in the pursuit of a single strategy. First, companies that are single-minded open themselves up to a single critical fault. Caterpillar, Inc. differentiated by manufacturing the highest-quality earthmoving equipment. However, Caterpillar was so preoccupied with precision and durability that it forgot about efficiency and economy and was undercut on price by Japanese firms by 30 percent. Second, if companies pursue specialized strategies, competitors can imitate them more easily than if they employ mixed strategies. Additionally, pure cost leadership can accelerate the move toward commodity markets where no competitor benefits.[14]

Another concern arises because of evidence that the pursuit of a pure generic strategy will not sustain a competitive advantage in hypercompetitive environments.[15] When the competitive environment changes rapidly, successful organizations must maintain flexibility. Pursuing a generic strategy within the arena of hypercompetition will only provide the firm with a temporary competitive advantage, the sustainability of which is dependent on a combination of customer needs, firm resources and capabilities, and the existence of isolating mechanisms.[16]

Value Disciplines

Treacy and Wiersema coined the term *value disciplines* to describe different ways successful companies can create value for customers. Specifically, they identify three different kinds of generic strategies that have successfully been used by companies such as Nike, Dell Computer, and Home Depot—*product leadership, operational excellence,* and *customer intimacy.*[17]

Companies pursuing *product leadership* typically produce a continuous stream of state-of-the-art products and services. Such companies are innovation-driven, and they constantly raise the bar for competitors by offering more value and better solutions. Compaq Computer is a company that creates value through product leadership.

Compaq has extended into new areas within the computer industry by utilizing product development to reduce its reliance on the PC market and improve its dwindling profit margins.[18] In 2000, Compaq Computer had revenues of $42 billion with a profit of $569 million. Of these revenue and profit totals, personal computer sales accounted for only 49 percent of revenues and 13 percent of profits. The balance of Compaq's revenues and profits came from computer servers, computer services, Web site development, computer storage, and corporate personal computing.

As part of its consumer product development, Compaq introduced products under the iPAQ brand. The iPAQ name allowed Compaq to develop a new identity for its new products. It offers consumers the reliability of the Compaq name with a fresh look. One new product is the Pocket PC, which is a wireless device that offers calendar, travel, e-mail, and music storage functions. Compaq has also introduced BlackBerry, a wireless e-mail device; the Personal Audio Player, a small portable MP3 player; and the Home Internet Appliance, a miniature desktop computer designed solely for Internet access.

Operational excellence—the second value discipline—describes a strategic approach aimed at better production and delivery mechanisms. Wal-Mart, American Airlines, and FedEx all pursue operational excellence.

Starwood Hotels & Resorts Worldwide also emphasizes operational excellence.[19] Starwood is one of the largest hotel chains in the world with 742 establishments in 80 countries including famous brands like the Sheraton, Westin, Four Points, and St. Regis. Following an extended period of subpar performance, the company decided to stylishly renovate its under-performing hotels and focus on doing and presenting everything it already did, much better.

The firm's biggest changes were made to the Sheraton hotel chain, which underwent a $750 million makeover. This renovation was undertaken to restore a reputation for reliability, value, and consistency. The revamping did away with flowered bedspreads in favor of a Ralph Lauren style. Practical amenities like ergonomic desk chairs and two-line telephones became standard.

Many of Starwood's Four Points brand underwent renovations with as much as 80 percent of the original hotel structure torn down. Every room was redesigned and redecorated. Twenty-four hour fitness facilities were opened. Olympic-sized heated swimming pools with outdoor reception areas became standard. Business centers were expanded to include ballrooms and meeting rooms to accommodate groups of all sizes. Management expanded dining options to range from restaurants to a pub. Guestroom hallways and lobbies were brightened and dramatically redesigned in a subtle, Mediterranean style. Wallpaper borders, sconce lighting, and artful signage were added to present the hotel with a bright fresh look.

Starwood's focus on operational excellence was immediately successful. For the four straight quarters following the activation of the changes, Starwood led Marriott and Hilton in North American revenue per available room. Operating income increased 26 percent.

A strategy based on *customer intimacy* concentrates on building customer loyalty. Nordstrom and Home Depot continually tailor their products and services to changing customer needs. Pursuing customer intimacy can be expensive, but the long-term benefits of a loyal clientele can pay off handsomely.

Because the vast majority of companies worldwide now claim to give top priority to customer concerns, it might be hard to imagine how a firm distinguishes itself through customer intimacy. Home Depot provides an excellent example of a firm that succeeded.[20] Home Depot uses customer intimacy initiatives to marginalize competitors.

The company's plan began with the creation of its Service Performance Initiative (SPI), which emphasizes changing daily operations to provide a more shopper friendly store atmosphere. Home Depot added off-hour stocking that moves merchandise in and out of inventory during late evening hours, or after closing for those stores that have not expanded their operating hours to 24 hours per day.

The main benefit of the new stocking method is the ability of employees to focus on customer service and sales. Before the implementation of the initiative, salespeople spent 40 percent of their time with customers and 60 percent on other work-related duties. Following SPI, they were able to spend 70 percent of their time with customers on sales-oriented tasks and 30 percent on other duties.

Home Depot undertook two additional customer intimacy initiatives. The first was the installation of Linux Info for point-of-sale support systems. The new system is capable of allowing customers to place orders from home over the Internet and have the purchase processed at the store's register. This process allows customers to enter the store simply for pickup having already purchased their merchandise. The second initiative involves home improvement classes taught at Home Depot stores. Customer intimacy is enhanced when courses teach customers how to buy and install the proper materials and construction equipment. Home Depot sells products and receives customer feedback as a result of the courses.

Most successful companies try to excel in one of the three value disciplines. Explicitly choosing a value discipline and focusing available resources on creating a gap between the company and its immediate competitors sharpen a company's strategic focus.

STRATEGIC ANALYSIS AT THE BUSINESS UNIT LEVEL

Process

The process of formulating competitive strategy at the business unit level is shown in Figure 4-3. It identifies four specific steps: (1) analyzing the competitive environment, (2) anticipating key competitors' actions, (3) generating formulating strategic options, and (4) choosing among the alternatives.

Step one, analyzing the competitive environment, deals with two questions: With whom do we compete, now and in the future? What relative strengths do we have as a basis for creating a sustainable competitive advantage? Answering these questions requires an analysis of the remote external environment, the industry environment, and internal capabilities. Step two, anticipating key competitors' actions, focuses on understanding how competitors are likely to react to different strategic moves. Industry leaders tend to behave differently from challengers or followers. A detailed competitor analysis is helpful in gaining an understanding of how competitors are likely to respond and why. Step three, identifying strategic options, requires a balancing of opportunities and constraints and a consideration of a diverse array of strategic options ranging from defensive to preemptive moves. Step four, choosing among alternatives, consists of narrowing the various options to a final choice. To assist in this process of formulating competitive strategy at the business unit level, we look at a number of widely used analytical frameworks.

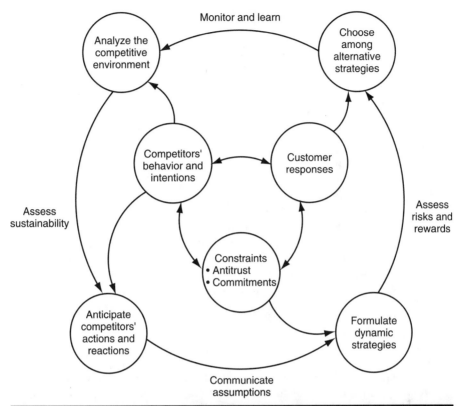

FIGURE 4-3   Formulating Business Unit Strategy

Source: *Wharton on Dynamic Competitive Strategy* by George S. Day and David J. Reibstein. Copyright © 1987 by John Wiley & Sons, Inc. This material is used by permission of John Wiley & Sons, Inc.

Profit Pool Analysis

An industry's *profit pool* is the total amount of profit earned at all points along the industry's value chain.[21] Analyzing who makes profit, where in the value chain, and why, is important to understanding industry economics. Profitability typically varies by customer group, product category, and geographic area or distribution channel. What is more, the pattern of profit distribution is often quite different from that of revenue concentration. In the automobile industry, for example, car manufacturing and distribution generate the highest revenues, but auto leasing, insurance, and auto loans are the most profitable activities. Mapping the industry's profit pool, therefore, provides important insight into profit potential. It also helps executives to understand how the industry is evolving by raising such questions as: Why have profit pools formed where they have? How is the profit distribution likely to change? Mapping a profit pool consists of four steps: (1) defining the pool's boundaries, (2) estimating its overall size, (3) allocating profits to the different value chain activities, and (4) verifying the results.

Analyzing Product/Market Scope

Growth vector analysis, depicted in Figure 4-4, is based on the recognition that a company can increase its strategic scope within an industry by offering more products/technologies/services and by tapping more customer segments. The group of product-market combinations that a firm serves defines its product/market scope. Further, growth *within* the current market scope is called *concentration,* growth by moving into related or new customer segments is referred to as *market development,* and growth into related or new products is *product/technology development.* A change in both customer segments served and products/technologies offered is called *diversification,* which we discuss in greater detail in the next chapter.

When analyzing alternative directions for growth, it is useful to perform a similar analysis for key competitors. The combined analysis allows executives to determine whether the original assumptions about growth, the business's competitive position, or the potential for improvement are still tenable, as well as to gain insight into competitors' intentions, and the way the specific product markets are evolving.

Companies that stay close to their current core competencies and concentrate their growth into related markets and products are more successful than companies that diversify widely. Therefore, it is strategically more attractive to consider growth into related products and segments before looking further afield.

Gap Analysis

Plotting alternative growth vectors for a company and its primary competitors often reveals *gaps* in the way a market is served, i.e., where industry sales are below their potential and the causes for such shortfalls. *Gap analysis*—the process of comparing an industry's market potential to the combined current market penetration by all competitors—can lead to the identification of additional avenues for growth. Figure 4-5 attempts to depict this process. Gaps between a market's potential and current sales levels can be the result of (1) product-line gaps—the unavailability of product versions for specific applications or usage occasions, (2) distribution gaps—overlooked customer segments that have difficulty accessing the product, (3) usage gaps—underdeveloped

---

FIGURE 4-4 Product/Market Scope Analysis

		Present products	Improved products	New products
Market Scope	Existing market	Concentration	Product extension	Product development
	Expanded market	Market extension	Market/product extension	Product development/ market extension
	New market	Market development	Product extension/ market development	Diversification

Product Scope

Source: *Marketing Management,* 6/E by Kotler, Phillip, © 1989. Reprinted by permission of Pearson Education, Inc., Upper Saddle River, NJ.

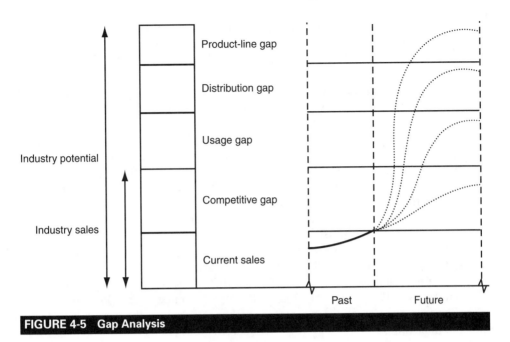

FIGURE 4-5   Gap Analysis

applications for the product, and (4) competitive gaps—opportunities to displace competitors with weak product entries or questionable performance.

Segmentation

Most executives are familiar with *market segmentation*—the process of dividing a market into relatively homogeneous, minimally overlapping segments that benefit from distinct marketing approaches. Whether done on the basis of demographics, buying patterns, or other data about products and customers, market segmentation helps tailor the specification and delivery of value to specific customer groups.

Strategic segmentation has a slightly broader focus: It focuses on identifying segments of an industry that offer the best prospects for long-term, sustainable results. It also considers the long-term defensibility of different segments by analyzing barriers to entry such as capital investment intensity, proprietary technologies and patents, geographical location, and tariffs and other trade barriers.

Competitor Analysis

Because of the ever-increasing complexity that characterizes industry evolution, many business assumptions are no longer tenable. The competitive realities of the new millennium are that markets are neither distinct nor their boundaries well-defined, competition is not mainly about capturing market share, customer and competitor profiles are constantly shifting, and competition occurs simultaneously at the business unit and corporate levels. These new realities call for executives to adopt a broader perspective on strategy and for them to ask new questions. Do consumer companies compete primarily at the business unit level, at the corporate level, or both? Do companies compete as stand-alone entities or as extended families that include their supplier bases?

When a firm defines its competition, should executives focus on the corporate portfolio of which the strategic business unit (SBU) is a part? What are the competitive advantages of a portfolio of businesses against stand-alone companies? Which is more important to sustainable competitive advantage, access to money or information technology?

As these questions suggest, competitive analysis must be paired with an analysis of the drivers of industry evolution. Consequently, strategies cannot be neatly compartmentalized at the SBU or corporate level. A principal rationale behind the concept of the diversified corporation is that the benefits of a portfolio transcend financial strength. A portfolio of related businesses reflects an integrated set of resources—core competencies that transcend business units—and has the potential for developing a sustainable corporate advantage that must be considered along with competitive considerations at the business unit level.

To analyze *immediate competitors,* five key questions are useful: (1) Who are our firm's direct competitors, now and in the future? (2) What are their major strengths and weaknesses? (3) How have they behaved in the past? (4) How might they behave in the future? (5) How will this affect our industry and company?

In many markets, it is possible to identify a *leader,* one or more *challengers,* and a number of *followers* and *nichers.* While labeling competitors risks erring on the side of simplicity, such an analysis provides further insight into the competitive dynamics of the industry.

Leaders tend to focus on expanding total demand by attracting new users, developing new uses for their product or service, or encouraging more use of existing products and services. Defending market share is important to them, but they may not wish to aggressively take more share from their immediate rivals because to do so can be more costly than expanding the market, or because they wish to avoid scrutiny by regulatory agencies. Coca-Cola, for example, is focused more on developing new markets overseas than it is on taking market share from Pepsi in the domestic market.

Challengers, on the other hand, typically concentrate on a single target—the leader. Sometimes they do so directly, as in the case of Fuji's challenge to Kodak. At other times, they use indirect strategies. Computer Associates, for example, acquired a number of smaller competitors before embarking on a directly competitive strategy with larger rivals.

Followers and *nichers* compete with more modest strategic objectives. Some followers use a strategy of innovative imitation, whereas others elect to compete selectively in a few segments or with a more limited product or service offering. Nichers typically focus on a narrow slice of the market by concentrating, for example, on specific end users in certain geographic areas, or by offering specialty products or services.

The identification of *potential* competitors is more difficult. Firms that are currently not in the industry but can enter at relatively low cost should be considered. So should companies for whom there is obvious synergy by being in the industry. Customers or suppliers who can integrate backward or forward comprise another category of potential competitors.

Product Life Cycle Analysis

In Chapter 2, we introduced the product life cycle concept in the context of analyzing how industries evolve. This concept is also useful as a benchmark for strategy development. As we have seen, the evolution of an industry or product class depends on the interaction of a number of factors including the competitive strategies of rival firms, changes in customer behavior, and legal and social influences. Because companies can affect the shape of the product life cycle, simple extrapolations of current growth trends are of limited value. What is useful, however, is to consider typical competitive responses to the changes that accompany the transition from a market's *emerging stage* to growth to maturity and, ultimately, to decline, as depicted in Figure 4-6.

A high level of uncertainty characterizes the emerging stage of a product or industry life cycle. Competitors often are unsure which segments to target and how. Potential customers are unfamiliar with the new product or service, the benefits it offers, where to buy it, or how much to pay. Consequently, a substantial amount of strategic experimentation is a hallmark of embryonic industries. *Growth* environments are less uncertain but competitively more intense. At this stage of an industry's evolution, the number of rivals is usually largest. Therefore, competitive shakeouts are common toward the end of the growth phase. *Mature* industries, though the most stable, are stagnant. Innovation can give rise to new spurts of growth in specific segments, technological breakthroughs can alter the course of market development and upset the competitive order, and global opportunities can open avenues for further growth. *Declining* industries are typically regarded as unattractive. Even here, however, clever strategies can produce substantial profits. We will return to these different scenarios in Chapter 5 when we consider specific strategies for each environment.

DESIGNING A PROFITABLE BUSINESS MODEL

Designing a profitable business model is a critical part of formulating a business unit strategy. Creating an effective model requires a clear understanding of how the firm will generate profits and of the strategic actions it must take to do so over the long term.

Adrian Slywotzky and David Morrison have identified 22 business models—designs that generate profits in a unique way.[22] They present these models as examples, believing that others do or can exist. The authors also confirm that in some instances profitability depends on the interplay of two or more business models. This research demonstrates that the mechanisms of profitability can be very different, but a focus on the customer is the key to the effectiveness of each model.

What is our business model? How do we make a profit? Slywotzky and Morrison suggest that these are the two most productive questions asked of an organization. The classic strategy rule suggested: "Gain market share and profits will follow." This approach once worked for most industries. However, as a consequence of competitive turbulence caused by globalization and rapid technological advancements, the once-popular belief in a strong correlation between market share and profitability has collapsed in many industries.

How can businesses earn sustainable profits? The answer is found by analyzing the following questions: Where will the firm be able to make a profit in this industry? How should the business model be designed so that the firm will be profitable? Slywotzky and Morrison describe the following profitability business models as ways to answer these questions. Each model fits with different business patterns and strategies to move a company into the profit zone.

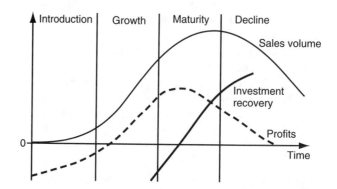

Characteristic	*Emerging*	*Growth*	*Maturity*	*Decline*
Concentration of competitors	High; few pioneers	Declining as more competition enters	Increasing after shakeout	High; few remaining harvesters
Product differentiation	Low, if any	Increasing; imitations and variations	High; increasing market segmentation	Decreasing as competitors leave market
Barriers to entry	High, if product can be protected	Decreasing; growing technology transfer	Increasing as capital intensity increases	High capital intensity, low returns
Barriers to exit	Low; little investment	Low, but increasing	High for large company	Decreasing; endgame
Price elasticity of demand	Inelastic, few customers	Increasingly elastic	Inelastic only in segments	Very elastic; bargaining power of buyers high
Ratio of fixed to variable cost	Generally low	Increasing	High	Decreasing
Economies of scale	Few, generally unimportant	Increasing capital intensity	High	High
Experience curve effects	Large early gains	Very high; large production volume	Decreasing magnitude	Few
Vertical integration of competitors	Low	Increasing	High	High
Risk involved in business	Low	Increasing	Increasing	Declining exit barriers

FIGURE 4-6   Strategic Choices Over the Product Life Cycle

Source: A. J. Rowe, R. O. Mason, K. E. Dickel, and N. A. Snyder, *Strategic Management: A Methodological Approach,* 3rd edition, 1989, Addison-Wesley Longman, Glenview, IL. Reprinted by permission.

1. *The Customer Development/Customer Solutions Profit model.*   Companies that use this business model make money by finding ways to improve their customers' economics and by investing in ways for customers to improve their processes.

2. *The Product Pyramid Profit model.*   This profit model is effective in markets where customers have strong preferences for product characteristics, including variety, style, color, and price. By offering a number of variations, companies can build so-called product pyramids. At the base are low-priced, high-volume products, and at the top are high-priced, low-volume products. The profit is concentrated at the top of the pyramid, but the base is the strategic firewall, i.e., a strong, low-priced brand that deters competitor entry, thereby protecting the margins at the top. Consumer goods companies and automobile companies use this model.

3. *The Multi-component System Profit model.*   Some businesses are characterized by a production/marketing system that consists of components that generate substantially different levels of profitability. In hotels, for example, there is a substantial difference between the profitability of room rentals and that of bar operations. In such instances, it often is useful to maximize the use of the highest-profit components to maximize the profitability of the whole system.

4. *The Switchboard Profit model.*   Some markets function by connecting multiple sellers to multiple buyers. The Switchboard Profit model creates a high-value intermediary that concentrates these multiple communication pathways through one point or switchboard and thereby reduces costs for both parties in exchange for a fee. As volume increases, so too do profits.

5. *The Time Profit model.*   Sometimes, speed is the key to profitability. This business model takes advantage of first-mover advantage. To sustain this model, constant innovation is essential.

6. *The Blockbuster Profit model.*   In some industries, profitability is driven by a few great product successes. This business model is representative of movie studios, pharmaceutical firms, and software companies, which have high R&D and launch costs and finite product cycles. In this type of environment, it pays to concentrate resource investments in a few projects rather than to take positions in a variety of products.

7. *The Profit Multiplier model.*   This business model reaps gains, again and again, from the same product, character, trademark capability, or service. Think of the value that Michael Jordan, Inc. creates with the image of the great basketball legend. This model can be a powerful engine for businesses with strong consumer brands.

8. *The Entrepreneurial Profit model.*   Small can be beautiful. This business model stresses that diseconomies of scale can exist in companies. This model is effectively used to attack companies that have become comfortable with their profit levels, with formal, bureaucratic systems that are remote from customers. As their expenses grow and customer relevance declines, such companies are vulnerable to entrepreneurs who are in direct contact with their customers.

9. *The Specialization Profit model.*   This business model stresses growth through sequenced specialization. Consulting companies have used this design successfully.

10. ***The Installed Base Profit model.*** A company that pursues this model profits because its established user base subsequently buys the company's brand of consumables or follow-on products. Installed base profits provide a protected annuity stream. Examples include razors and blades, software and upgrades, copiers and toner cartridges, and cameras and film.

11. ***The De Facto Standard Profit model.*** This is a variant of the Installed Base Profit model. It occurs when the Installed Base model becomes the de facto standard that governs competitive behavior in the industry, as is the case with Oracle.

NOTES

1. M. E. Porter, *Competitive Strategy: Techniques For Analyzing Industries And Competitors,* The Free Press, 1980, and M. E. Porter, *Competitive Advantage: Creating And Sustaining Superior Performance,* The Free Press, 1985.
2. A. M. McGahan and M. E. Porter, "How Much Does Industry Matter, Really?" *Strategic Management Journal,* 1997, 18: pp. 15–30.
3. R. P. Rumelt, D. E. Schendel, and D. J. Teece, *Fundamental Issues In Strategy,* Harvard Business School Press, 1994.
4. A. J. Slywotzky and D. J. Morrison, with B. Andelman, *The Profit Zone; How Strategic Business Design Will Lead You To Tomorrow's Profits,* New York: Times Books, 1997.
5. Slywotzky and Morrison, *The Profit Zone; How Strategic Business Design Will Lead You To Tomorrow's Profits,* Chap. 1.
6. B. T. Gale and R. D. Buzzell, "Market Position and Competitive Strategy," in *The Interface Of Marketing And Strategy,* G. Day, B. Weitz, and R. Wensley (Eds.), JAI Press, Inc., 1993.
7. R. D. Buzzell and B. T. Gale, *The PIMS Principles; Linking Strategy To Performance,* The Free Press, 1987.
8. A. Zimmerman, E. Spagat, and S. McCartney, "Southwest Airlines' Kelleher, Who Kept Costs Low and Morale High, Cuts Duties," *The Wall Street Journal,* March 20, 2001, p. A3.
9. M. E. Booth and G. Philip, "Technology, Competencies, and Competitiveness: The case for reconfigurable and flexible business strategies," *Journal of Business Research,* 1998, 41 (1): pp. 29–40.
10. R. B. Robinson, Jr. and J. A. Pearce, II, "Planned Patterns of Strategic Behavior and Their Relationship to Business-Unit Performance," *Strategic Management Journal,* 1988, 9 (1): pp. 43–60; A. I. Murray, "A Contingency View of Porter's 'Generic Strategies,'" *Academy of Management Review,* 1988, 13 (3): pp. 390–400.
11. C. W. L. Hill, "Differentiation Versus Low Cost or Differentiation and Low Cost: A Contingency Framework," *Academy of Management Review,* 1988, 13 (3): pp. 401–412.
12. D. Miller, "The Generic Strategy Trap," *The Journal of Business Strategy,* 1992, 13 (1): pp. 37–42.
13. J. A. Belohlav, "The Evolving Competitive Paradigm," *Business Horizons,* 1996, 39 (2): pp. 11–19.
14. D. Nath and S. E. Newell, "Organizational Responses to a Hypercompetitive Environment: A Case Study of Pepsi Canada," *Journal of Business Research,* 1998, 41: pp. 41–48.
15. R. Veliyath and E. Fitzgerald, "Firm capabilities, business strategies, customer preferences, and hypercompetitive arenas: The sustainability of competitive advantages with implications for firm . . . ," *Competitiveness Review,* 2000, 10 (1): pp. 56–82.
16. M. Partridge and L. Perren, "Developing Strategic Direction: Can generic strategies help?" *Management Accounting,* 1994, 72 (5): pp. 28–30.
17. M. Treacy and F. Wiersema, "Customer Intimacy and Other Value Disciplines," *Harvard Business Review,* Jan.–Feb. 1993, pp. 84–93.

18. E. Nee, "Refocusing Compaq," *Fortune,* March 5, 2001, pp. 128–134; G. Marcial, "Not the Compaq We Used to Know," *Business Week,* March 6, 2001.

19. C. Binkley, "From Orange Shag to Pinstripes: Sheraton Chain Gets a Makeover," *Wall Street Journal,* April 19, 2000, p. B1; D. Brady, "At Starwood, the CEO Is in the Details," *Business Week,* November 20, 2000, pp. 142–144.

20. P. Bond, "Home Depot Divides Tasks to Improve Service," *Milwaukee Journal Sentinel,* February 25, 2001, p. F3; W. M. Bulkeley, "Linux, Maverick of Computing, Gets Respectable," *The Wall Street Journal,* April 9, 2001, p. B1; C. Terchune, "Home Depot Inc. Expands Web Sales Across 48 States," *The Wall Street Journal,* April 27, 2001, p. B8.

21. O. Gadiesh and J. L. Gilbert, "Profit Pools: A Fresh Look at Strategy," *Harvard Business Review,* May–June 1998, pp. 139–147; O. Gadiesh and J. L. Gilbert, "How to Map Your Industry's Profit Pool," *Harvard Business Review,* May–June 1998, pp. 149–162.

22. A. J. Slywotzky and D. J. Morrison, *The Profit Zone; How Strategic Business Design Will Lead You To Tomorrow's Profits.*

Business Unit Strategy: Context and Special Dimensions

INTRODUCTION

Generic strategies are useful for identifying broad frameworks within which a competitive advantage can be developed or exploited. However, to forecast the relative effectiveness of different options, strategists consider the *context* in which a strategy is to be implemented. To see how such analysis is done, we examine six types of industry settings in this chapter. First, we look at three contexts that relate to the various evolutionary stages of an industry: *introduction, growth, mature,* and *declining.* We then discuss three additional industry environments that pose unique strategic challenges: *fragmented, deregulating,* and *hypercompetitive.* Because hypercompetition is increasingly characteristic of business-level competition in many industries, we then discuss two critical attributes of successful firms in dynamic industries: speed and innovation. We conclude this chapter by considering the importance of vertical integration and horizontal thinking in business unit strategy formulation.

EMERGING, GROWTH, MATURE, AND DECLINING INDUSTRIES

Strategy in Emerging Industries

New industries or industry segments emerge in a variety of ways. Technological breakthroughs can launch entirely new industries or re-form old ones, as in the case of changes to the telephone industry with the advent of cellular technology. Sometimes changes in the macro environment can spawn new industries. Examples are solar energy and Internet technology.

From a strategic perspective, new industries present new opportunities. Their technologies are typically immature. This means that competitors will actively try to improve upon existing designs and processes, or leapfrog them altogether with next-generation technology. A battle for standards might ensue. Costs are typically high and unpredictable, entry barriers are low, supplier relationships are underdeveloped, and distribution channels are just emerging.

Timing can be crucial in determining strategic success in an emerging market. The first company to come out with a new product or service often has a *first-mover advantage.* First movers have the opportunity to shape customer expectations and define the competitive rules of the game. In high-technology industries, first movers can sometimes set standards for all subsequent products. Microsoft was able to accomplish this with its Windows operating system. In general, first movers have a relatively brief window of opportunity to establish themselves as industry leaders in terms of technology, cost, or service.

Strategically, it is crucial to assess the chance a company has to exercise leadership in the emerging market as a way to reduce risk. In addition to the ability to shape the industry structure based on timing and method of entry, and experience in similar situations, leadership opportunities include the ability to control product and process development through superior technology, quality, or customer knowledge; the ability to leverage existing relationships with suppliers and distributors; and the ability to leverage access to a core group of early, loyal customers.

Strategy in an Industry's Growth Stage

Growth presents a host of challenges. Competitors tend to focus on expanding their market shares. Over time, buyers have become knowledgeable and now better distinguish between competitive offerings. As a result, increased segmentation often accompanies the transition to market maturity. Cost control becomes an important element of strategy as unit margins shrink, and new products and applications are harder to find. In industries with a global potential, international markets become more important. The globalization of competition also introduces new uncertainties as a second wave of global competitors enters the race.

Strategically, there are other new factors to watch as well. Whereas during the early growth phase companies tend to add more products, models, sizes, and flavors to appeal to an increasingly segmented market, toward the end of the growth phase cost considerations become a priority. Additionally, process innovation becomes an important dimension of cost control, as do the redefinitions of supplier and distributor relations. Finally, horizontal integration becomes attractive as a way of consolidating a company's market position or increasing a firm's international presence.

Competing companies that enter the market at this time, often labeled *followers,* have different advantages than early market leaders. Later entrants have the opportunity to evaluate alternative technologies, delay investment in risky projects or plant capacity, and imitate or leapfrog superior product and technology offerings. Followers also tap into proven market segments rather than take the risks associated with trying to develop latent market demand into ongoing revenue streams.

Firms that consider entry into a growing industry must also face the strategic decision of whether to enter through internal development or acquisition. Entry into a new segment or industry through *internal development* involves creating a new business, often in a somewhat unfamiliar competitive environment. It is also likely to be slow and expensive. Developing new products, processes, partnerships, and systems takes time and requires substantial learning. For these reasons, companies increasingly are turning to *joint ventures, alliances,* and *acquisitions* of existing players as strategies for invading new product-market segments.

Two major issues must be analyzed as part of the decision process to enter a new market: (1) What are the structural barriers to entry? (2) How will incumbent firms react to the intrusion? Some of the most important structural impediments, as discussed in Chapter 2, are the level of investment required, access to production or distribution facilities, and the threat of overcapacity.

Potential retaliation is harder to analyze. Incumbents will oppose a new player if resistance is likely to pay off. This is more likely to occur in mature markets if growth is low, products or services are not highly differentiated, fixed costs are high, capacity is ample, and the market is of great strategic importance to incumbents. However, the likelihood of competitor resistance at any stage of the life cycle suggests that the search for new markets should focus on industries that are experiencing some disequilibria; where incumbents are likely to be slow to react; where firms can influence the industry structure; and where the benefits of entry exceed the costs, including the costs of dealing with possible retaliation by incumbents.[1]

Strategy in Mature and Declining Industries

Carefully choosing a balance between differentiation and low-cost postures, and deciding whether to compete in multiple or single industry segments, are critically important issues as maturity sets in and decline threatens. Growth tends to mask strategic errors and lets companies survive; a low- or no-growth environment is far less benevolent.

Firms earn attractive profits during the long maturity stage of an industry's growth when they do the following: (1) concentrate on segments that offer chances for higher growth or higher return, (2) manage product and process innovation aimed at further differentiation, cost reduction, or rejuvenating segment growth, (3) streamline production and delivery to cut costs, and (4) gradually harvest the business in preparation for a strategic shift to more-promising products or industries.

Counterbalancing these opportunities, mature and declining industries contain a number of strategic pitfalls that companies should avoid: (1) an overly optimistic view of the industry or of the company's position within it, (2) a lack of strategic clarity shown by a failure to choose between a broad-based and a focused competitive approach, (3) investing too much for too little return—the so-called cash trap, (4) trading market share for profitability in response to short-term performance pressures, (5) unwillingness to compete on price, (6) resistance to industry structural changes or new practices, (7) placing too much emphasis on new product development compared to improving existing ones, and (8) retaining excess capacity.[2]

Exit decisions are often extremely difficult, in part because exiting might be actively opposed in the marketplace. Possible exit barriers include government restrictions, labor and pension obligations, and contractual obligations to other parties. Even if a business can be sold—in part or as a whole—there are a host of issues to address. The negative effects of an exit on customer, supplier, and distributor relations, for example, can ripple throughout the entire corporate structure if the firm is an SBU of a larger corporation. In this case, shared cost arrangements can produce cost increases in other parts of the business; and labor relations can become strained, thereby diminishing the strategic outlook for the corporation as a whole.

Industry Evolution and Functional Priorities

The requirements for success in industry segments change over time. Strategists need to use these changing requirements as a basis for identifying and evaluating a firm's strengths and weaknesses. Figure 5-1 depicts four stages of industry evolution and the changes in functional capabilities that are often associated with business success at each stage.[3] At a minimum, it suggests dimensions that are particularly deserving of in-depth consideration when a strategic assessment is undertaken.

The early development of a product market typically entails slow growth in sales, major R&D emphasis, rapid technological change in the product, operating losses, and a need for sufficient resources or slack to support a temporarily unprofitable operation. Success at this emerging stage is often associated with technical skill, with being first in new markets, and with having a marketing advantage that creates widespread awareness.

Rapid growth brings new competitors and reorders the strengths necessary for success. Brand recognition, product differentiation, and financial resources to support both heavy marketing expenses and price competition become key strengths.

As the industry moves through a shakeout phase and into the maturity stage, sales growth continues, but at a decreasing rate. The number of industry segments increases, but technological change in product design slows considerably. As a result, competition usually becomes more intense, and promotional or pricing advantages and differentiation become key internal strengths. The rate of technological change in process design accelerates as the many competitors seek to provide the product in the most efficient manner. Whereas R&D is critical in the emerging stage, efficient production is now crucial.

When the industry moves into the decline stage, strengths center on cost advantages, superior supplier or customer relationships, and financial control. Competitive advantage can exist at this stage if a firm serves gradually shrinking markets that competitors are choosing to leave.

FRAGMENTED, DEREGULATING, AND HYPERCOMPETITIVE INDUSTRIES

Strategy in Fragmented Industries

Fragmented industries are those in which no single company or small group of firms has a large enough market share to strongly affect the industry structure or outcomes. Many areas of the economy share this trait—including retail sectors, distribution businesses, professional services, and small manufacturing firms. Fragmentation seems to be most prevalent when entry and exit barriers are low, there are few economies of scale or scope, cost structures make consolidation unattractive, products or services are highly diverse or need to be customized, and close, local control is essential.

Thriving in fragmented markets can require creative strategizing. Focus strategies that creatively segment the market based on product, customer, type of order/service, or geographic area, combined with a no-frills posture, can be effective. Sometimes, scale and scope economies are hidden, await new technological breakthroughs, or are not well recognized because the attention of the players has been elsewhere. In such instances, creative strategy can unlock these hidden sources of advantage and dramatically change the dynamics of the industry. The entrepreneurial ventures of H. Wayne Huizinga are prime examples.

FIGURE 5-1 Stages of Industry Evolution and Functional Priorities of Business Strategy

Stage of Industry Evolution

Functional Area	Introduction	Growth	Maturity	Decline
Marketing	Resources/skills to create widespread awareness and find acceptance from customers; advantageous access to distribution	Ability to establish brand recognition, find niche, reduce price, solidify strong distribution relations, and develop new channels	Skills in aggressively promoting products to new markets and holding existing markets; pricing flexibility; skills in differentiating products and holding customer loyalty	Cost-effective means of efficient access to selected channels and markets; strong customer loyalty or dependence; strong company image
Production operations	Ability to expand capacity effectively, limit number of designs, develop standards	Ability to add product variants, centralize production, or otherwise lower costs; ability to improve product quality; seasonal subcontracting capacity	Ability to improve product and reduce costs; ability to share or reduce capacity; advantageous supplier relationships; subcontracting	Ability to prune product line; cost advantage in production, location, or distribution; simplified inventory control; subcontracting or long production runs
Finance	Resources to support high net cash overflow and initial losses; ability to use leverage effectively	Ability to finance rapid expansion, to have net cash outflows but increasing profits; resources to support product improvements	Ability to generate and redistribute increasing net cash inflows; effective cost control systems	Ability to reuse or liquidate unneeded equipment; advantage in cost of facilities; control system accuracy; streamlined management control

Personnel	Flexibility in staffing and training new management; existence of employees with key skills in new products or markets	Existence of an ability to add skilled personnel; motivated and loyal work force	Ability to cost effectively reduce work force, increase efficiency	Capacity to reduce and reallocate personnel; cost advantage
Engineering and research and development	Ability to make engineering changes, have technical bugs in product and process resolved	Skills in quality and new feature development; ability to start developing successor product	Ability to reduce costs, develop variants, differentiate products	Ability to support other grown areas or to apply product to unique customer needs
Key functional area and strategy focus recovery	Engineering: market penetration	Sales: consumer loyalty; market share	Production efficiency; successor products	Finance; maximum investment

Source: From J. A. Pearce II and R. B. Robinson, Jr., *Strategic Management: Strategy Formulation, Implementation and Control*, 8th edition, 2003. R. D. Irwin, Inc.: Chicago, IL. chapter 5.

Wall Street was distinctly skeptical when Huizinga took Waste Management Corporation public in 1971 and explained that he would acquire hundreds of mom-and-pop garbage companies using stock as his principal currency. He planned to exploit differences in public and private valuation and, by placing these smaller entities under single management, unlock hidden value. At the time of its initial public offering, Waste Management had a capitalization of $5 million. When Huizinga departed in 1984, its market value was $3 billion.

Huizinga got the same initial reception when he took control of Blockbuster in 1987. By taking a similar strategic approach to the one that had transformed the waste disposal industry, Huizinga grew Blockbuster's market capitalization from $32 million to $8.4 billion in 1994, when he sold the company to cable giant Viacom.[4]

Strategy in a Deregulating Environment

Deregulation has reshaped a number of industries in recent years. Some interesting competitive dynamics take place when artificial constraints are lifted and new entrants are allowed to enter. Perhaps the most important has to do with the timing of strategic moves. U.S. experience shows that deregulating environments tend to undergo considerable change twice—once when the market is opened and again about five years later.[5]

Deregulation in the United States became a major issue in 1975 when the Securities and Exchange Commission abolished fixed rates for U.S. securities brokers. Deregulations quickly followed in airlines, trucking, railroads, banking, and telecommunications. In each instance, a more or less similar pattern developed:

1. Immediately following the opening of the market, a large number of new entrants rushed in; most failed within a relatively short period of time.
2. Industry profitability deteriorated rapidly as new entrants, often operating from a lower cost basis, destroyed industry pricing for all competitors.
3. The pattern of segment profitability was altered significantly—segments that once were attractive became unattractive because too many competitors entered, while previously unattractive segments suddenly became more interesting from a strategic perspective.
4. The variance in profitability between the best and worst players increased substantially, reflecting a wider quality range of competitors.
5. Two waves of merger and acquisition activity ensued—a first wave focused on consolidating weaker players, and a second wave among larger players aimed at market dominance.
6. After consolidation, only a few players remained as broad-based competitors; most were forced to narrow their focus to specific segments or products in a much more segmented industry.

Deregulation of energy markets in the United States provides excellent examples of how competitors face both loss and opportunity. Deregulation of the energy industry in 1996 caused economic hardship for many of California's electric power companies. In 2001, Pacific Gas and Electric, California's largest investor-owned utility, reported $9 billion of debt and filed for bankruptcy.[6] Two primary reasons account for the bankruptcy of the once-leading retail electricity company. First, PG&E incurred billions of dollars of debt that it was not allowed to pass along as costs to its customers. Utility companies, including PG&E, were forced to pay high rates to wholesalers. However, because of deregulatory measures, they were not allowed to charge the retail price to consumers. Second, a provision of the deregulation disallowed the company from expanding its power generators to other regions of the state. Therefore, power had to travel longer distances and accrued added costs for the utility company along the way.

PG&E filed for Chapter 11 bankruptcy, arguing that government regulators did not move swiftly to resolve the crisis that has caused multiple blackouts and cost the state billions of dollars. By taking their case to court, PG&E hoped to erase some of the $9 billion debt that it owed wholesalers and to try to reverse regulations that do not allow the company to increase retail rates.

Strategically, deregulation poses a host of challenges for companies. Joel Bleeke identifies four distinct strategic postures that prove successful in coping with the turmoil associated with deregulation: (1) broad-based distributors that offer a wide range of products and services over a large geographic area, (2) low-cost entrants that develop into niche players, (3) focused segment marketers that emphasize the company's value added to specific, loyal customer groups, and (4) shared utilities that focused on making economies of scale available to smaller competitors.[7]

Broad-based distribution companies that understand the challenges associated with fending off a flood of low-cost upstarts take early pricing actions, eliminate cross subsidies between products or segments, and conserve resources for protracted battles in a deteriorating environment. For example, following deregulation, AT&T quickly reduced prices to high-volume business customers to counter MCI's and Sprint's aggressive marketing efforts. It also cut about 20 percent of its work force to match the cost structure of the new entrants. AT&T conserved capital by cutting back on new market development and acquisitions to prepare for the inevitable future rainy day.

Low-cost entrants are typically catalysts for change in a deregulating environment. Few such entrants, however, can successfully stake out a sustainable position based on low cost alone. Most survivors tend to become specialty or niche players over time. The key strategic choices they have to make are deciding the segments to target—taking on broad-based competitors in their core markets may not be the best choice—and deciding on a migration route toward their specialty or niche status.

Focused segment marketers target value-added segments from the outset. Their staying power often depends on the strength of their relationships with their customers. Accordingly, the principal strategic challenges facing focused segment marketers include (1) identifying new approaches for strengthening relationships with customers—for example, by developing customer information systems and databases, (2) leveraging segment strength into entry into related segments or product categories, and (3) upgrading products and services to lock in existing customers.

Shared utilities define a fourth strategic group in a deregulated environment. Their profit strategy is to provide low-cost entrants with economies of scale by sharing costs among many companies. Telerate, for example, provides worldwide, instant government bond and foreign exchange quotations to a range of small- and medium-size traders, allowing them to compete more effectively with their larger rivals.

Shared utilities are essential to the evolution of the industry but a shakeout among competing utilities is often unavoidable. The battle among different airline reservations systems is a good illustration. At most, a few will ultimately survive. As likely, one will become the de facto industry standard.

Strategy in Hypercompetitive Industries

Hypercompetitive industries are characterized by intense rivalry. Successful strategies are often based on taking competitors by surprise, for example, by introducing a product when least expected, and then moving on as the competition tries to recover. *Hypercompetitive* strategies, therefore, are designed to enable the company to gain an advantage over competitors by disrupting the market with quick and innovative change. The goal is to neutralize previous competitive advantages and create an unbalanced industry segment.[8]

The intense rivalry in a hypercompetitive environment often results in short product life cycles, the emergence of new technologies, competition from unexpected players, repositioning by current players, and major shifts in market boundaries. Personal computers, microprocessors, and software all frequently experience the effects of hypercompetition. The telecommunications industry also provides many examples. Commonly, hypercompetitive strategies involve the bundling of services—such as local calling, long-distance calling, Internet access, and even television transmission—to retain current customers and acquire new ones.

In a hypercompetitive market, successful companies are able to manipulate competitive conditions to create advantage for themselves and destroy the advantages enjoyed by others. Within their dynamic and ever-changing environment, firms that stand to benefit are those possessing three major qualities: rapid innovation and speed, superior short-term strategic focus, and market awareness.

Speed and innovation are the foremost requirements for success in a hypercompetitive environment. The focus of companies is on gaining temporary advantage, achieving short-term profitability, and then quickly shifting their strategic focus before competitors can react effectively. It is crucial that hypercompetitive companies be able to innovate rapidly and then follow up on that innovation with equally quick manufacturing, marketing, and distribution of their products. In this manner, they are able to rapidly shift the industry dynamics and gain market share at a pace that exceeds that of the competition. Without speed as an attribute, a company is at a severe disadvantage because competitors will capitalize on market opportunities first, costing it valuable market share.

The second characteristic of successful hypercompetitive firms is superior short-term strategic focus. Firms that have the ability to manipulate the competition into making long-term commitments will find the hypercompetitive marketplace beneficial.

The final requirement for success in a hypercompetitive environment is strong market awareness. Firms must be able to understand consumer markets to deliver high-impact products and provide superior standards of customer support. Having strong customer focus allows firms to identify a customer's needs while uncovering new and previously untapped markets for their products. Once the needs of the customer are identified, firms win temporary market share through a redefinition of quality.

The traditional concept of sustainable competitive advantage is centered on the belief that long-term profitability can be achieved through segmented markets and low to moderate levels of competition. However, strategists now recognize another requirement: Over the long term, sustainable profits are possible only when entry barriers restrict competition. Evidence from the current business environment is that business models that are dependent on these conditions have a sharply declining rate of success, principally because of hypercompetition. Continuous erosion and re-creation of competitive advantage have come to characterize many industries with companies seeking to disrupt the status quo and gain a temporary profitable advantage over larger competitors.

BUSINESS UNIT STRATEGY: SPECIAL DIMENSIONS

Speed

Speed is emerging as a pivotal critical success factor in an expanding variety of industries, especially those characterized by transitional or habitual hypercompetition.[9] Coupled with trends toward globalization, the multiplying business applications of the Internet have led to the elevation of speed as a strategic priority. The unprecedented growth in business-to-consumer and business-to-business Internet connections is refashioning commerce and the U.S. economy. The importance of speed now rivals quality and customer orientation in most markets. Yet, it is the newest and least understood of the critical success factors. It therefore receives special attention in this chapter.

In a competitive context, *speed* is the pace of progress that a company displays in responding to current or anticipated business needs. It is gauged by a firm's response times in meeting customer expectations, in innovating and commercializing new products and services, in changing strategy to benefit from emerging market and technological realities, and in continuously upgrading its transformation processes to improve customer satisfaction and financial returns.

Responding to industry challenges to increase their customer responsiveness are *speed merchants* that built their strategies on the rapid pace of their operations. Their accelerated change activities become a hallmark for the progress of the industry. Speed merchants modify their environments to convert their core competencies into competitive advantages. As a consequence, competitive landscapes are altered in their favor.

The public images of a growing number of firms are synonymous with the speed that they exhibit: AAA with fast emergency road service, Dell with fast computer assembly, Domino's with fast pizza delivery, and CyberGate with fast Internet access. A critical assessment of the strategies of these high-profile companies provides three important insights: (1) There are distinct and identifiable sources of pressure that create the demand on a company to accelerate its speed. (2) An emphasis on speed places new cost, cultural, and change process requirements on a company. (3) Several implementation methods have been proven to accelerate a firm's speed of operations.

Figure 5-2 presents a model to guide executives in the acceleration of their companies' speed. It reminds us that pressures to increase company speed can be both externally and internally generated. Firms can assume a reactive posture and await an increase in speed by competitors before making their own investment, or they can gamble on a payoff from a proactive move to improve.

Pressures to Speed

Speed is almost universally popular. Customers in nearly every product-market segment seek immediate need satisfaction, and they reward quick-acting companies with market share growth. Because employees of speed-oriented companies enjoy the

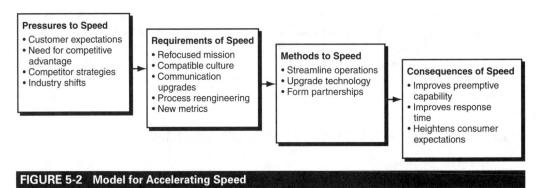

FIGURE 5-2   Model for Accelerating Speed

Source: Reprinted from *Organizational Dynamics,* 2002, 30 (3), John A. Pearce II, "Speed Merchants," pp. 1–16, Copyright © 2002, with permission from Elsevier Science.

job flexibility and heightened individual responsibility that are required to maintain the strategy, they reward their employers with the loyalty and commitment that is so highly prized in competitive environments. Suppliers to fast-moving companies are willing to bear extra costs and responsibilities to earn partnerships with firms that seem destined to overtake competitors that conduct business in time-tested rather than time-conscious ways.

Pressures for speed come from customers' expectations, from competitors who accelerate their own pace, from the company itself when it seeks to establish a new competitive advantage, and from the adjusting priorities of a changing industry. These pressures for speed often seem to blend into a seamless force. However, different sources of pressure can be most effectively addressed with a specifically targeted company strategy. Therefore, strategic planners' correct anticipation or recognition of the specific source of pressure helps to assure that their investments in new speed will provide maximum returns.

Experience has shown that there are four principal sources of pressure for increasing speed:

1. *Customers.*   Customers demand responsiveness. The consumer quality movement of the past two decades has been trumped by a new emphasis on getting quality products and services quickly.
2. *Basis of competitive advantage.*   Increasing the speed with which products are innovated, developed, manufactured, and distributed has been associated with the success of firms in establishing a new competitive advantage and important cost benefits.
3. *Competitive pressures.*   Competitive viability often mandates changes for the acceleration of speed. When facing intense competitive pressures, speed is often one of the few options for a company to choose to differentiate its offering.
4. *Industry shifts.*   Speed is particularly important to survival in industries characterized by short product life cycles. Global competition, exponential advancements in technology, and shifting customer demands combine to produce shorter life cycles and the need for faster product development.

Requirements of Speed

As a strategic weapon, a speed initiative requires that every aspect of an organization be focused on the pace at which work is accomplished. Executives must foster a fast culture within their organizations. The agility that comes from a speed orientation and carefully tailored resource investments provides the prerequisite competitive means to change and accelerate a firm's strategic course. Specifically, action must be taken on the following issues: refocusing the business mission, creating a speed-compatible culture, upgrading communications within the business, focusing business process reengineering, and committing to new performance metrics.

Refocusing the Business Mission   When the board and officers articulate a long-term vision of a speed-oriented company, the mission statement serves as a basis for shared expectations, planning, and performance evaluation regarding the increase in speed throughout the organization.

Creating a Speed-Compatible Culture   Speed is facilitated in a company by nurturing an organizational culture that is conducive to speed and by adopting an evaluation system that rewards those who can increase aspects of organizational speed. Change management techniques, including total quality management (TQM), benchmarking, time-based competition, outsourcing, and partnering can each play a role in focusing an organization on increasing facets of its overall speed.

Upgrading Communication   The increase in speed requires dramatically upgraded methods for clear and timely communication. Increasingly, all parties expect instantaneous communication between customers, manufacturers, suppliers, and service providers.

Refocusing Business Process Reengineering (BPR)   BPR is undertaken to reorganize a company to eliminate barriers that create distance between employees and customers. It involves fundamentally rethinking and redesigning a process to enable a customer focus to permeate all phases of business activity. The deployment of employees is evaluated to determine how they can best contribute. Upgrading employee involvement, not eliminating employees, is the true intent of BPR.

Committing to New Performance Metrics   A specific set of metrics has proven valuable in gauging a firm's progress in improving performance from its investments in speed. The metrics include sales volume, innovation rate, customer satisfaction, processing time and cost controls, and marketing specifics including innovation support, learning, and initiatives.

Methods to Speed

The development of speed as a competitive advantage begins with an internal analysis by a firm to determine where speed exists and where it does not. Companies then look to quickly eliminate any speed gaps. Three categories of methods dominate corporate option lists: streamlining operations, upgrading technology, and forming partnerships.

Streamlining Operations   Many companies enter new markets with a level of competitive information that would have traditionally been labeled as insufficient to support investment. However, most of these firms are not marginalizing quality; they have adopted a new strategic scheme. With a speed-enhanced ability to obtain quick post-implementation feedback from the marketplace and to respond with unparalleled speed in making adjustments, successful innovations no longer need to be flawless at introduction.

Upgrading Technology   Using the latest informational technologies (ITs) to create speed, companies are able to roll out new product information faster. The common goal of speed-focused IT is to connect manufacturers with retailers to enhance information sharing, and to streamline and accelerate product distribution. In turn, shortening pipelines speeds products to shelves and satisfies customers with less costly inventories. Doubling back, technology enables companies to learn customers' buying patterns to better anticipate their preferences.

Forming Partnerships   Sharing business burdens is a proven way to shorten the Pert chart for improving market responsiveness, i.e., partners collapse time. Ford Motor Company's partnership with General Motors and DaimlerChrysler provides a front-page example. The three major auto manufacturers joined to develop an Internet portal that links their purchasing organizations with 30,000 raw material suppliers. These Web-based exchanges also increase the speed with which the automobile companies respond to customer inquiries at every stage along the supply chain.

The evidence from business practice supports the emergence of speed as a critical success factor and as a primary element in business unit strategy. The company goal of accelerating speed to satisfy consumer needs is becoming less of an option and more of a mandate for financial survival. Fortunately, businesses can be systematic in evaluating the pressures and requirements for change that they face in accelerating their speed. Methods available for implementing upgrades are becoming quickly established and are backed by the records of success faster firms enjoy.

Creating Value Through Innovation

Value creation often depends on innovation. Many companies find that profitable growth requires more than judicious acquisitions or careful subtractions by shedding unprofitable operations or downsizing. They recognize a need to generate more value from core businesses and to leverage core competencies. These strategic initiatives, in turn, increase the demand for innovation.[10]

Creating a culture of innovation eludes many companies because it transcends traditional strategic planning practices. Strategic planning too often centers on existing or closely related products and services rather than on opportunities to drive future demand. In contrast, innovation is a product of anticipating, assessing, and fulfilling potential customer needs in a creative manner. Sometimes it is technology-based, but often it springs from the firm's recognition of explicit or latent customer needs. Innovation can be directed at any point in the customer or company value chain, from sourcing raw materials to value-added, after-sale services.

Although many businesses pursue innovation, for almost 100 years Minnesota Mining & Manufacturing (3M) has succeeded because its business model is based on a culture that is geared to producing innovative products. Best known for Post-It Notes, Scotchgard, and Scotch Tape, 3M's business segments include industrial, transportation, graphics and safety, healthcare, consumer and office, electronics and communications, and specialty materials. In 2000, 3M's three largest segments contributed 61 percent of sales and 68 percent of operating income.[11] Research and new product development accounted for 6.6 percent of sales in 2000, which is 160 percent higher than the average for the industry.

Because of the company's unparalleled success as an innovator, its approach deserves broader consideration. Fundamentally, six mandates drive innovation at 3M:

1. *Support innovation from research and development to customer sales and support.*
2. *Understand the future by trying to anticipate and analyze future trends.*   3M has developed a program called Foresight in which industry experts survey the remote and external environments for changes in technology and other trends in order to identify new market opportunities, called *greenfields.*
3. *Establish stretch goals.*   This driver is important to 3M because it is a measure that encourages growth. One example of a stretch goal is the new-product sales target. This target is that 40 percent of sales will be from products introduced in the past four years. In addition, 10 percent of sales will be from products introduced in the current year.
4. *Empower employees to meet goals.*   At 3M this is accomplished through its 40-year-old 15-percent rule. This gives 3M researchers the opportunity to devote 15 percent of their time to any creative idea or project, and management approval is not required.
5. *Support broad networking across the company.*   This driving force calls for the sharing of discoveries within the company. A 3M corporate policy states that technologies belong to the company, which signals that research results are to be shared across all of its six business segments.
6. *Recognize and reward innovative people.*   An innovative program at 3M rewards innovative people through peer-nominated award programs and a corporate hall of fame.

Fostering a culture of innovation takes time and effort. Although there is no universal model for creating an innovating environment, a look at successful companies reveals certain common characteristics. First, a business needs a *top-level commitment to innovation.* Commitment to innovation is evident in the attitudes of top executives, through their communication of belief in the benefits of innovation to all levels of the organization, and in their willingness to sponsor and guide new product activity.

Second, a business needs a *long-term focus.* "Quarteritis," the preoccupation with the next quarter's results, is one of the most common stumbling blocks to innovation. Innovation is an investment in the future, not a rescue mission for current top- or bottom-line problems.

Third, a business needs a *flexible organization structure.* Innovation rarely flourishes in a rigid structure, with complicated approval processes, or with bureaucratic delays and bottlenecks.

Fourth, a business needs a combination of *loose and tight planning and control.* Allocating all direct, indirect, overhead, and other costs to a development project virtually guarantees its demise. Few innovative ideas can immediately be translated into commercial ventures that cover all of their own costs or meet conventional payback requirements.

Finally, to create an environment for innovation, a business needs to include a system of *appropriate incentives.* Reward systems in many companies are oriented toward existing businesses, with short-term considerations outweighing longer-term innovation and market development objectives. Innovation can flourish only when risk-taking is encouraged, occasional failure is accepted, and managers are held accountable for missing opportunities as well as exploiting them.

VERTICAL INTEGRATION

Decisions about vertical scope are of key strategic importance at the business unit level because they involve the decision to redefine the domains in which the firm will operate. When does backward integration to secure access to raw materials or other supplies pay off? When is forward integration that is undertaken to gain access to retail customers worth the costs, risks, and broadening of focus that are involved?

The issue of vertical integration is fundamental to strategic choice. It defines the extent to which and how companies participate in an industry's value chain. Vertical integration therefore affects industry structure and competitive intensity. In the oil industry, for example, there are companies that are fully integrated from exploration to refining and marketing, whereas others specialize in one or more upstream or downstream stages of the value chain.

The comparative analysis of a large number of businesses in a variety of industries in the PIMS study raises three important questions: (1) Are highly integrated businesses in general more or less profitable than less integrated ones? (2) Under what circumstances is a high level of vertical integration likely to be most profitable? (3) Apart from their influence on overall profitability, what are the principal benefits and risks associated with vertical integration strategies?[12]

The answers are intriguing. With respect to the first question—How profitable is vertical integration?—the study found that for both industrial and consumer manufacturing businesses *backward* integration generally raised ROI but *forward* integration did not. The study results also showed that partial integration generally hurt ROI. The findings indicate that the effect of vertical integration on profitability varies with the size of the business. Larger businesses tend to benefit to a greater extent than smaller ones. This suggests, in answer to the second question, that vertical integration may be a particularly attractive option for businesses with a substantial market share in which further backward integration has the potential of enhancing competitive advantage and increasing barriers to entry. Finally, with respect to question three—What other factors should be considered?—there is evidence that suggests that alternatives to ownership such as long-term contracts and alliances should actively be considered, vertical integration almost always requires substantial increases in investment, and projected cost reductions do not always materialize, but that vertical integration sometimes results in increased product innovation.

Though useful as a general guide to crafting strategy, it is important to note that some of these findings need to be validated for application to a specific industry.

HORIZONTAL STRATEGIC THINKING

Whereas business unit strategy focuses on *how* to compete in a particular industry, corporate strategy is about selecting *which* industries should be chosen as arenas for competition. Clearly, the two are related. In fact, the boundaries between the two have become increasingly permeable, reflecting the growing realization that the relation-ships among strategic business units and between different SBUs and corporate head-quarters are important determinants of corporate and competitive advantage. The term *horizontal thinking* is often used to describe coordinating mechanisms aimed at unlocking value based on synergies between different parts of the corporate portfolio.

Horizontal thinking gained prominence as strategists moved away from diversifi-cations based simply on financial synergies. Disappointing performance with this approach led companies to focus more on *related* diversification, which meant that more attention is paid to issues of fit between different business units in the portfolio and between the businesses and corporate headquarters. Horizontal thinking also received a push when the emphasis further shifted from growth to performance. The technology revolution both increased the potential for performance synergies and made them more achievable. Finally, as markets become more global, companies increasingly compete as much at the corporate level as they do at the business unit level, often in multiple industries. Procter & Gamble, Kimberly-Clark, Scott Paper, and Johnson & Johnson compete with each other in multiple lines of business. In some industries, corporations compete in one business unit, are each other's customers in another, and have alliances in a third. In short, business unit strategy and corporate strategy are more closely related than ever before.

This close relationship is reflected in the planning processes used in most large, diversified corporations. Even though we can speak of separate strategies at the corpo-rate and business unit levels, the process by which these strategies are generated increasingly reflects their interdependence. Strategy development at the corporate level focuses on the composition and management of the corporate portfolio, whereas business unit strategy centers on attaining and maintaining a competitive advantage at the business unit level.

The message for business-level executives is clear. SBU strategies must serve two agendas. Except in rare instances when financial synergy is the overriding objective of the parent corporation, a business unit must succeed in satisfying the demands of its own stakeholders while simultaneously contributing directly and distinctly to the needs of the corporation. In this sometimes-schizophrenic world of the semiautonomous busi-ness unit, SBU executives must balance two sets of priorities. But, successful strategists are also candidates to double-dip in the reward pool.

NOTES

1. M. E. Porter, *Competitive Strategy: Techniques for Analyzing Industries and Competitors,* The Free Press, 1980, Chapters 11, 12.
2. Porter, *Competitive Strategy: Techniques for Analyzing Industries and Competitors.*
3. J. A. Pearce, II and R. B. Robinson, Jr., *Formulation, Implementation and Control of Competitive Strategy,* 8th edition, Chicago: Irwin/McGraw-Hill, 2003, Chapter 5.
4. A. E. Serwer, "Huizinga's Third Act," *Fortune,* August 5, 1996; "Waste Management, Inc."; *Notable Corporate Chronologies,* Gale

Research, Inc., 1996; and T. Ferguson, "Off-the-shelf-autos, A Chat with J. David Power III," *Forbes,* February 10, 1997.
5. J. E. Bleeke, "Strategic Choices for Newly Opened Markets," *Harvard Business Review,* Sept.–Oct. 1990.
6. M. L. Holson, "California's Largest Utility Files for Bankruptcy," *The New York Times,* April 7, 2001, p. 1; M. L. Holson, "Bankruptcy Filing of California Utility Tests the Limits of the Court," *The New York Times,* April 9, 2001, p. 1.

7. Bleeke, "Strategic Choices for Newly Opened Markets."

8. R. A. D'Aveni, "Strategic Supremacy Through Disruption and Dominance," *Sloan Management Review,* 1999, 40 (3).

9. J. A. Pearce, II, "Speed Merchants," *Organizational Dynamics,* 2002, 30 (3): pp. 1–16.

10. C. A. de Kluyver, "Innovation: The Strategic Thrust of the Nineties," *A Cresap Insight,* July 1988.

11. W. E. Coyne, "How 3M Innovates for Long-Term Growth," *Research Technology Management,* March–April 2001, pp. 21–24.

12. R. D. Buzzell and B. T. Gale, *The PIMS Principles; Linking Strategy To Performance,* The Free Press, 1987.

CHAPTER

The Dynamics of Corporate Strategy

INTRODUCTION

Formulating a corporate strategy is the process of creating a blueprint for the long-term direction of a diversified company. A number of today's global 1,000 companies are larger than the economies of entire nations. These corporations are typically engaged in several different businesses and have a global reach. Executives of each of these corporations make strategic choices regarding businesses and markets to enter. The impacts of the strategies they implement extend beyond their corporations. Frequently, these decisions have consequences for entire economies, and in some instances, the fate of citizens around the world. The importance of corporate strategy is magnified by the difficulty of formulating and implementing the plans that can provide satisfaction of stakeholder claims. The difficulty arises from a multitude of internal, competitive, and situational factors that interact to create a dynamic, complex, and uncertain environment in which corporate strategies are formulated.

The contemporary corporate strategy framework has its roots in the mistakes of the past. It reflects the now-discredited conglomerate deals that gave rise to such unwieldy companies as ITT Corporation and Litton Industries and destroyed more shareholder value than they created. It takes account of the lessons from the debt-laden leveraged buyouts and breakups, and it explains why senior executives in many industries became preoccupied with growth by acquisition and unleashed a global wave of mergers.

Indeed, if there is one constant in the history of corporate strategy, it is the quest for size. Grow bigger or be swallowed has become the de facto corporate mantra in many boardrooms. As we begin a new century, the value of all announced mergers and acquisitions continues to increase each year. Leading the new wave of consolidations are companies, including banks, healthcare providers, computer software companies, and media, telecommunications, and entertainment giants, that believe that they have learned from the mistakes of the past and need size to prosper.

We begin our discussion by taking a look at the concepts of the *economics of scale and scope*—two fundamental underpinnings of corporate strategy—and try to answer the question: Is bigger better? Next, we turn to the context in which corporate strategy is developed. In particular, we note the importance of the dispersion in the ownership of large corporations and of the emergence of the market for *corporate governance*. With this background, we trace the evolution of strategic thinking at the corporate level. We conclude the chapter with four perspectives on corporate strategy formulation—the *portfolio, value-based,* and *resource-based* points of view—and assess their relative merits.

THE ECONOMICS OF SCALE AND SCOPE

The Logic of Managerial Enterprise

Alfred D. Chandler, the well-known business historian, argued that, "to compete globally, you have to be big."[1] Looking back over a century of corporate history, he noted that the logic of managerial enterprise begins with economics—and the cost advantages that come with scale and scope in technologically advanced capital-intensive industries. Large plants frequently produce products at a much lower cost than can small ones because the cost per unit decreases as volume goes up *(economies of scale)*. In addition, larger plants can use many of the same raw and semifinished materials and production processes to make a variety of different products *(economies of scope)*. What is more, these principles are not limited to the manufacturing sector. Procter & Gamble, through its multibrand strategies, benefits from economies of scope because of its considerable influence at the retail level. As a service example, the scale and scope economies of the major accounting firms have enabled them to dominate the auditing services market for large companies by displacing a number of respectable local and regional accounting firms.

Size alone, however, is not enough to guarantee competitive success. To capitalize on the advantages that scale and scope can bring, companies must make related investments to create global marketing and distribution organizations. They must also create the right management infrastructure to effectively coordinate the myriad activities that make up the modern multinational corporation.

Timing Is Key

The timing of strategic moves is critical. It is no accident that IBM, Intel, Microsoft, Hoechst, and Sony—all dominant in their industries—were *first movers*. First mover advantage explains why American hardware and software companies were successful in building a global presence, and why Japanese corporations seized the advantage in many electronics industries. Challengers face a formidable uphill battle. They must build productive capacity while first movers are perfecting their production processes, developing marketing and distribution organizations to compete for market share in already established markets, and attracting managerial talent capable of beating entrenched competitors.

The Diversification Movement

The logic of managerial enterprise—the right combination of scale and scope economics, marketing and distribution power, management structure, and first mover advantage—still guides corporate strategy. Its indiscriminate application, however, has cost shareholders dearly. When misapplied, the logic of corporate growth can turn size from a competitive asset into a liability.

The misguided diversification movement provides ample evidence. Facing stronger competition from abroad and diminished growth prospects in a number of traditional industries, many U.S. companies began moving into industries in which they had no particular competitive advantage. Believing that general management skill could offset knowledge gained from experience in an industry, executives thought that because they were successful in their own industries they could be just as successful in others. A depressing number of their subsequent experiences showed that these executives overestimated their relevant competence and, under these circumstances, bigger was worse, not better. Unrelated conglomeration was detrimental to shareholder wealth.

Research by the Ashridge Strategic Management Center suggests that most multi-business corporations destroy shareholder value in at least part of their portfolio.[2] Four causes of value destruction are cited: (1) negative effects of central executive influence on the companies, (2) the pursuit of elusive synergies in constructing a portfolio of businesses, (3) the constraining behavior of corporate staffs, and (4) inopportune acquisitions. This does not mean that opportunities to realize economies of scale and scope should be ignored. Rather, these findings suggest that bigger is not always better and that a trade-off exists between size and the organizational complexity in running a global, multibusiness corporation.[3]

The 1990s: Consolidation in the Face of Globalization

The decade of the 1990s witnessed a global wave of consolidation. The drivers of deregulation and globalization put the quest for scale and scope at the top of corporate strategic agendas in many industries. Corporate executives and directors, as well as their counterparts in the financial community, attempted to heed the lessons of the past and to stick closer to the logic of managerial enterprise. Early combinations, such as the 1991 merger of Chemical Bank Corporation and Manufacturers Hanover Corporation, seemed to signal that the Age of Reason in mergers and acquisitions had begun. The WorldCom-MCI merger was also a trendsetter because the combined entity was the first major company since AT&T that was capable of offering long-distance and local telephone service across the United States.

Other notable combinations were the union between Compaq Computer and Digital Equipment Corporation and the DaimlerChrysler merger. By taking over Digital, Compaq transformed itself from a PC maker into a full-line information systems and service company that was capable of competing with IBM, H-P, and Sun in the higher-end markets that it could not serve before. Similarly, the DaimlerChrysler combination changed the competitive dynamics of the global auto industry. By combining forces, Daimler, Germany's biggest industrial concern, and Chrysler, America's No. 3 carmaker, could offer a full product line around the globe. However, this merger is about more than cutting costs and filling product and geographic gaps. It is about the emergence of a new category of global carmaker at a critical moment in the industry, since worldwide plant capacity exceeds worldwide projections of car sales by more than 15 million vehicles each year.

History shows that large mergers in general, and high-tech combinations in particular, have a tendency to derail. Fusing the different corporate cultures and product lines may take years—an eternity in the hypercompetitive high-tech world. Yet, the early returns on the deals of the last decade are encouraging, reflecting a strategic perspective focused on synergies of operation, economies of scale, and global market clout, and not burdened by the oppressive debt levels that characterized the doomed combinations of the seventies.

One thing is clear: Size has once again become a priority in corporate strategy formulation. Furthermore, because few companies can rely on internal sources of growth alone, mergers, acquisitions, joint ventures, and alliances, despite their uneven track record, have become major instruments of corporate strategy.

STRATEGY AND CORPORATE GOVERNANCE

Ownership Patterns

In the beginning of the twentieth century, large U.S. corporations were controlled by the notorious captains of industry. Wealthy entrepreneurs—Morgan, Rockefeller, Carnegie, and DuPont—not only owned the majority of the stock in companies such as Standard Oil and U.S. Steel, they also exercised their rights to run these companies.

By the 1930s, however, the ownership of U.S. corporations had become much more widespread. Capitalism in the United States had made a transition from the *entrepreneurial model* to *managerial capitalism,* a model in which ownership and control had been separated. Effective control of the corporation was no longer exercised by the legal owners of equity—the shareholders—but by hired, professional managers.

With the rise of institutional investing in the 1970s, primarily through private and public pension funds, the responsibility of ownership became once again concentrated in the hands of a relatively small number of institutional investors who act as fiduciaries on behalf of individuals. This large-scale institutionalization of equity, which continues 30 years later, brought further changes to the corporate governance landscape. Because of their size, institutional investors effectively own a major fraction of many large companies. In addition, because investors' liquidity is restricted, they must protect their investments through active monitoring of the companies in which they invest. This modern model of corporate governance, which emphasizes monitoring over trading, is described as *fiduciary capitalism.*[4]

Relationship of Corporate Governance to Strategy

For the greater part of the 20th century, when managerial capitalism prevailed, executives had a relatively free rein in interpreting their responsibilities toward the various corporate stakeholders and, as long as the corporation made money and its operations were conducted within the confines of the law, they enjoyed great autonomy. Boards of directors, mostly selected and controlled by management, intervened only infrequently, if at all. Indeed, for the first half of the last century, corporate executives of many publicly held companies managed with little or no outside control. Serious problems surfaced, including unimpressive corporate earnings, exorbitant executive compensation, disappointing corporate earnings, and ill-considered acquisitions that amounted to little more than empire building that had the unintended consequence of depressing shareholder value.

The resulting risk-averse, internally focused, and self-satisfied executive teams of many companies increased their firms' external vulnerability. Taking advantage of the opportunity to capture underutilized assets, takeovers surged in popularity. Terms such as *leveraged buyout, dawn raids, poison pills,* and *junk bonds* became household words, and individual corporate raiders including Carl Icahn, Irwin Jacobs, and T. Boone Pickens became well known. The resulting takeover boom woke up sleepy boards, exposed underperforming companies and unlocked shareholder value. In the process, it helped to more closely align the incentives of management with those of shareholders.

The takeover era ended abruptly.[5] As capital dried up, junk bond–financed, highly leveraged hostile takeovers faded from the stage. Of lasting importance from this era was the emergence of institutional investors who knew the value of ownership rights, had fiduciary responsibilities to use them, and were big enough to make a difference.[6]

The past decade saw more gradual change. As boards found themselves under much closer scrutiny, directors started to take their oversight roles more seriously. Major shareholders, particularly institutional investors using their growing leverage, began to play a more active role in the governance process. The result has been a wave of structural and procedural reforms aimed at making boards more responsive, more proactive, and more accountable.

The changes in corporate governance have combined with the rise of global competition to redefine the way senior executives approach corporate strategy. CEOs have shown greater discipline in shaping corporate strategy, in part because they are reminded on a daily basis of their accountability to boards of directors, shareholders, and other stakeholders. It is also no coincidence that turnover among CEOs at major public corporations is at an all-time high, as stockholders are more demanding of high performance than ever before. In combination, the current competitive environment demands greater strategic focus, a global perspective, and superb leadership skills.

THE EVOLUTION OF STRATEGIC THINKING AT THE CORPORATE LEVEL

Early Perspectives

Earlier work on corporate strategy focused on the importance of building a *distinctive competence* that would provide the corporation with a competitive advantage in its various businesses, on the evolution of the *multidivisional* organizational structure that accompanied the conglomerate boom of the sixties, and on the need to create a *fit* between structure and strategy so that structure followed strategy.[7]

As corporations continued to add to the product-market-technology offerings, priorities for corporate diversification became a more pressing issue. A well-known study by Richard Rumelt examined the relationship between corporate performance and the degree of *relatedness* among its various businesses.[8] It identified three categories of relatedness based on their *specialization ratio,* the proportion of revenues derived from the largest single group of related businesses: *dominant business companies, related business companies,* and *unrelated business companies.* Dominant companies such as General Motors and IBM derive a majority of their revenues from a single line of business. Related business companies such as General Foods, Eastman Kodak, and DuPont diversify beyond a single type of business but maintain a common thread of relatedness throughout their portfolio. The components of the portfolios of unrelated business companies, or diversified conglomerates, have little in common. Rockwell International and Textron are examples of conglomerates that lack synergistic possibilities in products, markets, or technologies. The study concluded that companies with closely related portfolios outperform widely diversified corporations. This finding is important because it explains performance in terms of *synergy* among related businesses, an intuitive notion for many executives.

The BCG Approach to Portfolio Analysis

By the mid-1970s, most large corporations had diversified, primarily through acquisition. Corporate executives struggled with formulating a coherent strategy for their diverse array of semiautonomous divisions about which they often knew little. The well-known *growth/share matrix,* introduced by the Boston Consulting Group (BCG), helped executives confront these issues.[9]

The BCG approach to portfolio analysis is based on the observation that multidivision, multiproduct companies have a distinct advantage over nondiversified companies, specifically, the ability to channel resources into the most productive units. A diversified company can use the strength of one division to fuel the expansion of another. This ability to integrate investment patterns between different businesses makes it possible to optimize the performance of the portfolio as a whole rather than focus on the performance of individual units. To achieve this optimal allocation of resources, the BCG approach recognizes a role for each of a corporation's strategic business units, and integrates these roles into one overall portfolio approach. Product roles are assigned on the basis of a unit's cash flow potential and cost position relative to its principal competitors. Differences in growth and in cash flow potential determine how funds are allocated across the portfolio.

The analysis begins with the construction of a *growth/share matrix* for the company and its major competitors. Each business unit is plotted on a two-dimensional graph according to the relative market share it commands and the growth rate that characterizes its market, as shown in Figure 6-1.

Although placement of business units on the matrix is usually done subjectively, it is possible to enhance the sophistication of the model. To maximize the model's potential, a business unit can be indicated by a circle, the size of which is proportional to the annual dollar sales of the total market. A segment of the circle can then be shaded to indicate the firm's relative market share.

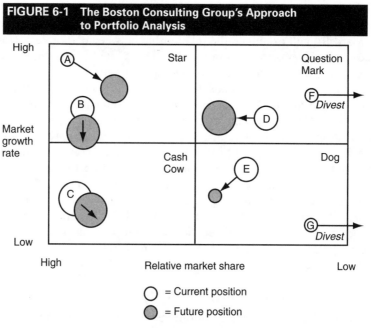

FIGURE 6-1   The Boston Consulting Group's Approach to Portfolio Analysis

Source: © The Boston Consulting Group. Reprinted by permission.

It is also possible to be more specific about the proper placement of a firm within a quadrant. High-growth markets typically show growth rates of more than 10 percent per year, and high-share products occupy a leadership position in their markets, i.e., they have a relative market share of at least 1.0. Therefore, the midpoints on the vertical and horizontal axes can be shown as 0.10 and 1.00, respectively.

The BCG matrix is divided into four quadrants, each representing a different growth/share position. *Question marks* are low-share/high-growth products. They typically offer new products with potentially large future sales volumes. Substantial cash investments are needed to improve their share position from one of a me-too entry to one of market leadership. *Stars* are high-growth/high-share products that might or might not be self-sufficient in terms of their cash needs. If handled successfully, they are the company's future cash cows. *Cash cows* are high-share/low-growth products that generate large amounts of cash—far more than they can profitably reinvest and therefore a source of funds. *Dogs* are low-share/low-growth products; they neither generate nor require much cash. Because some level of reinvestment is needed, and because returns are usually modest at best, they are often cash traps.

As conceptualized by the Boston Consulting Group, the way products move across the chart over time reflects the strategic moves by the company and the evolutionary forces acting on the industry. For example, if only share-maintenance level investments are made, market forces will cause all products to move downward and to eventually end up as dogs. The major strategic task, therefore, is redirecting excess cash generated by cash cows to fund market share increases for the most promising products in the portfolio—selected question marks whose positions are strong enough for them to become stars. Under this philosophy, question marks with a relatively weak competitive position should be divested or continued under a "no cash in" doctrine. Dogs can remain in the portfolio as long as they contribute to cash flow and do not tie up disproportionate amounts of working capital that can be put to better use.

These perspectives on strategy are based on the finding that high market share and profitability are strongly correlated in many stable market situations. Market dominance, therefore, becomes an appropriate strategic goal in high-growth markets, and maximizing cash generation is desirable in low-growth markets where market share gains are more costly to obtain. How many and which products to select for growth depend on their relative competitive strengths, the cost of gaining market leadership, and the cash flow generated by other products in the portfolio.

Experience-curve effects are an important factor in explaining the correlation between market share and profitability. For many manufacturing businesses, for example, a large percentage of the variances in profitability can be explained by competitive cost differentials that reflect differences in competitors' experience. The company with the largest cumulative volume of production often has the lowest unit cost, which translates into higher cash flow.

The assumption of a strong correlation between market share and profitability is not always justified, however, and therefore must be applied with care. Poor investment decisions can erode a market leader's capacity to generate cash. Experience in related products or a technology—the so-called shared experience—is sometimes as important as direct experience. Additionally, for service companies, experience effects may be less pronounced.

General Electric Business Screen

Shortly after the Boston Consulting Group pioneered its portfolio approach, General Electric and McKinsey & Company developed a slightly more complex matrix. Shown in Figure 6-2, the *General Electric Business Screen* uses nine cells to describe a company's portfolio. Its dimensions are each composites of several important factors. Instead of classifying a market based only on growth rate, it uses long-term *industry attractiveness,* which is defined to include such factors as the industry's growth rate, investment intensity, technological intensity, governmental influences, and other regulatory factors. Also, instead of characterizing a business's position in terms of market share alone, it defines *business strength* in terms of market share, technical strength, management cohesiveness and depth, and access to financial resources. Based on the intersection of a firm's ratings on industry attractiveness and business strength, the Business Screen prescribes growth/investment, selective investment/earnings, or harvesting/divestment strategies.[10]

Life-Cycle Matrix

Another variant of the portfolio methodology that has gained some currency was developed at Arthur D. Little, Inc. This *life-cycle matrix approach* plots businesses based on the stage of an industry's evolution and the strength of the company's competitive position, as shown in Figure 6-3.[11]

Limitations of Portfolio Analysis

Although portfolio analysis is useful in describing the current portfolio of a corporation, it has a number of limitations. First, labeling businesses is dangerous, especially as cash cows or dogs, since it can lead to self-fulfilling prophecies; milking a cash-cow business will almost certainly limit its growth, and classifying a business as a dog can discourage creativity in charting its future.

Second, portfolio analysis has prescriptive limitations. It does not answer such questions as: How do we grow overall revenues? What new businesses should be added to the portfolio?

Finally, as ownership of large corporations dispersed and shares became traded more freely, the assumption that companies should be self-sufficient in capital, a central premise of the BCG matrix, lost its validity. New options had to be considered such as paying out excess free cash flow to shareholders in the form of dividends and raising additional investment funds in the capital markets. At the same time, the rapid growth in the corporate headquarters staffs at many corporations prompted investors to ask what value these corporate resources contributed to the semiautonomous operations of the divisions.

The Value-Based Approach

Changes in the competitive environment set the stage for the emergence of the *value-based approach* to corporate strategy, with its focus on maximizing shareholder value. This approach treats strategic business units as separate entities that are valued according to their cash flow. It raises such questions as: How much economic value is created by each division? What is the optimal structure of the corporation? In effect, the value-based approach imputes a *share price* for each business unit. If the market

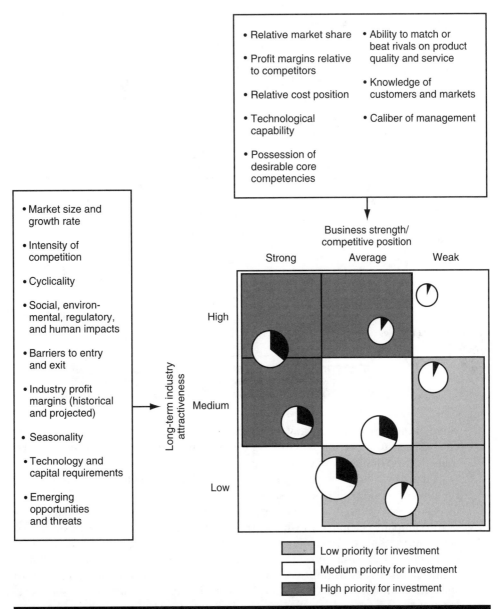

FIGURE 6-2   General Electric's Business Screen

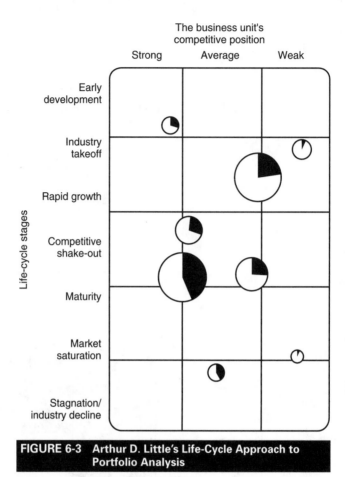

FIGURE 6-3 Arthur D. Little's Life-Cycle Approach to Portfolio Analysis

value of the corporation as a whole is less than the sum of the valuations of the different business units, action is required, often in the form of a sell-off of those business units that are implicitly undervalued.

Figure 6-4 shows the pentagon framework that depicts the value-based approach.[12] It shows several levels of analysis, starting with internally available data and restructuring options within the current portfolio. In the first step, the current market valuation of the company is compared with an objective assessment of the value of the company generated with its current corporate strategy. If the as-is discounted cash flow analysis of the current portfolio produces a higher value than shareholders are willing to pay, management needs to improve its communications with shareholders. Moreover, to show its confidence in its corporate strategy, it must consider moves such as a share repurchase program. If the internally developed cash flow analysis shows that the company is overvalued by the market, it might mean shareholders are anticipating a possible takeover or breakup. This outcome is a clear warning signal that management needs to revisit its corporate strategy and improve shareholder value.

Depending on the outcome of the overall valuation of the company, it is logical to consider strategic and operating improvements within the current portfolio as the second

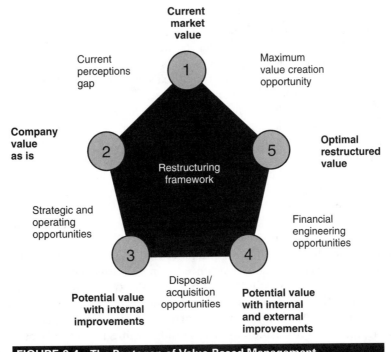

FIGURE 6-4   The Pentagon of Value-Based Management

Source: Valuation: Measuring and Managing the Value of Companies, by Tom Copeland, Tim Keller, and Jack Murrin. Copyright © John Wiley & Sons, Inc. This material is used by permission of John Wiley & Sons, Inc.

step. Such improvements can be targeted at the business unit level, for example, by focusing on increasing sales growth and operating margins or by decreasing working-capital requirements. At the corporate level, improvements can include reducing overhead or reexamining the strategies for managing the portfolio. If the problems uncovered at this stage are manageable, simple turnaround strategies involving one or more business units are appropriate. If the problems are pervasive, or if they can be dealt with better by a different corporate parent, more drastic action might be needed.

If straightforward business unit improvements or a turnaround strategy is not likely to improve shareholder value sufficiently, portfolio adjustments must be considered as the third step. As part of this process, management must revisit the rationale for the corporation's diversified posture. Portfolio adjustments to consider include shrinking the scope of the company's activities—through sell-offs, spin-offs, and liquidations—or expanding it. Expansion strategies, designed principally to complete or complement a related diversification strategy, can take various forms. *Vertical integration, horizontal integration,* and *cooperative strategies* are intriguing considerations.

The fourth and final step in the value-based approach involves *financial engineering* of the reconfigured corporate portfolio. Among the options that have provided troubled corporations with increased value for their shareholders are recapitalization, tax-favorable reorganization of global ownership structures, and changes in the corporation's debt-to-equity ratio.

The Resource-Based View of Strategy

In their influential article, "The Core Competence of the Corporation," C. K. Prahalad and Gary Hamel argued that strategies should build core capabilities that transcend the boundaries of traditional business units.[13] They urged corporations to center their portfolios on *core businesses* and adopt goals and processes aimed at enhancing *core competencies.* This core competency perspective was later extended to what is known today as the *resource-based view* (RBV) of the firm. The theory's central thesis is that a corporation is a collection of tangible assets, intangible assets, and organizational capabilities that collectively defines its distinctive competence. Thus, corporate strategy should center on the creation of value through the configuration and coordination of a set of multimarket activities.

Instead of focusing on synergies between component businesses, the RBV emphasizes the importance of a fit between corporate resources and product markets. The three sides of the triangle—*resources; businesses;* and *structure, systems, and processes*—represent the foundations of a strategy. When aligned in pursuit of a *vision,* and motivated by the right *goals* and *objectives,* a *corporate advantage* can be created that justifies the corporation's existence as a multibusiness entity.[14]

Although there are differences between the two perspectives, the core competencies and RBV approaches are highly compatible. It is difficult if not impossible to construct a cohesive corporate portfolio without paying attention to synergy among the various businesses. Shareholder value is always a primary objective. Furthermore, to be sustainable, competitive advantage at the corporate level must reflect a fit among shared resources, developing competencies, and the product markets in which it competes.

Contemporary Perspective

Current thinking about corporate strategy, while influenced by the RBV, integrates multiple approaches. It holds that companies should focus on how to create *value* through the *configuration* and *coordination* of its multimarket activities. The basic premise is that value creation is the fundamental purpose of corporate strategy, and the components of a multibusiness corporation should be synergistic.

To justify its existence as a multibusiness entity, a corporation must contribute to the competitive advantage of its individual businesses by shaping its portfolio and by coordinating its multimarket activities. Said another way, a corporation adds value by deciding which businesses it, rather than some other company, should own and why. The corporation must also develop the supporting management philosophy, processes, and organizational structure to generate superior performance in its individual businesses.

Analysis of Strategic Fit Among Businesses

The synergy among businesses in a portfolio can take a variety of forms. In the Boston Consulting Group's approach to portfolio planning, *strategic fit* is primarily defined in terms of financial characteristics—the ability of business units to generate or productively use cash. Other approaches to portfolio analysis argue that broadly defined functional skills such as distribution or manufacturing are critical to synergy. Complementary asset structures and skill sets can also define attractive opportunities—for example, when a transaction-intensive business such as claim processing is paired with information technology skills. Therefore, executives should look for fit among firms in their corporation's portfolio under three classifications: operating, market, and management.

Operating Fit

Sustained competitive advantage is often created by a fit among skills and resources, and the product markets in which they are applied. Fit can reside within specific businesses, as in the case of R&D capabilities, or it can take the form of core competencies that transcend the boundaries of business units such as Sony's ability to miniaturize or Honda's core competency in small engines. A related form of operating fit can occur when the business models for different business units have common and synergistic characteristics, e.g., when there is a high degree of similarity in critical success factors, such as specialties in brand development or manufacturing processes.

Market-Related Fit

When a corporation can create similarities in the markets that it serves—in customers, buying behavior, and distribution patterns—it can enhance its competitiveness. The essential requirement is that such fit translates into economies of scale or scope, or strengthens a company's position with suppliers, partners, distributors, or customers.

Management Fit

The realization of potential synergies among markets, resources, and operations depends on the presence of management fit between the corporate parent and its component businesses. Assessing management fit involves the identification of the critical success factors associated with each of the businesses in the portfolio, the assessment of the focus of improvements in each of the businesses, and the evaluation of how well the skills of the parent corporation fit with the value-enhancement efforts of each business unit. Irrespective of the degree of fit among portfolio businesses and with the parent organization, value is only created when potential synergies are *realized* and translated into corporate advantage as evidenced by enhanced, sustained performance.

NOTES

1. A. D. Chandler, "The Enduring Logic of Industrial Success," *Harvard Business Review,* March–April 1990, pp. 130–140.
2. A. Campbell and D. Sadtler, "Corporate Breakups," *Strategy & Business,* Booz Allen & Hamilton, 1998 (12): pp. 64–73.
3. P. C. Davis and A. Kamra, "The Value of Big in Banking," *Strategy & Business,* Booz Allen & Hamilton, 1998, (12): pp. 7–9.
4. J. P. Hawley and A. T. Williams, *The Rise of Fiduciary Capitalism in the United States,* Philadelphia: University of Pennsylvania Press, 2001.
5. Emily Thornton, "The Bids Sure Are Getting Hostile: Unsolicited offers are on the rise in a market ripe for consolidation," *Business Week,* January 14, 2002. Hostile takeovers made a dramatic comeback after the 2001–2002 economic recession. In 2001, the value of hostile takeovers climbed to $94 billion, more than twice the value in 2000 and almost $15 billion more than in 1988, the previous peak year.
6. R. Romano, *Politics and Pension Funds,* The Manhattan Institute, 1994.
7. A. Chandler, *Strategy And Structure,* MIT Press, 1960.
8. R. P. Rumelt, *Strategy, Structure, and Economic Performance,* Cambridge: Harvard University Press, 1974.

9. "Note on the Boston Consulting Group Concept of Competitive Analysis and Corporate Strategy," Harvard Business School, 1975.

10. *Strategic Management in GE,* Corporate Planning and Development, General Electric Corporation.

11. C. D. Hofer and D. Schendel, *Strategy Formulation: Analytical Concepts,* St. Paul: West Publishing, 1978.

12. T. Copeland, T. Keller, and J. Marrin, *Valuation: Measuring and Managing the Value of Companies,* McKinsey & Company, New York: John Wiley & Sons, 1995.

13. C. K. Prahalad and G. Hamel, "The Core Competence of the Corporation," *Harvard Business Review,* May–June 1990, pp. 79–91.

14. D. J. Collis and C. A. Montgomery, *Corporate Strategy; Resources And Scope of the Firm,* Homewood, IL: Irwin, 1997.

CHAPTER

7

Strategic Options at the Corporate Level

INTRODUCTION

In this chapter we identify the major strategic options at the corporate level. We begin with a discussion of *growth strategies*. This section covers concentrated growth strategies, diversification, mergers, acquisitions, and the cooperative strategies of joint ventures and alliances. We then briefly review the *disinvestment strategies* including retrenchment, sell-offs, spin-offs, and liquidations. Next, we consider the issue of *corporate management* and how a management style affects portfolio composition. We conclude the chapter with a discussion of *how to evaluate* strategy choices at the corporate level.

GROWTH STRATEGIES

Concentrated Growth Strategies

Concentrated growth is the strategy of a corporation that continues to direct its resources to the profitable growth of a single product line, in a delimited market, possibly with a dominant technology.[1] A small sample of corporations that implement concentrated growth strategies includes Allstate, Amoco, Apple Computers, Avon, Caterpillar, KFC, John Deere, Hyatt Legal Services, Goodyear, Giant Foods, Mack Truck, Martin Marietta, McDonald's, Swatch, Tenant, and TruGreen ChemLawn.

Concentrated growth often leads to enhanced performance. The abilities to assess market needs, develop detailed knowledge of customer behavior and price sensitivity, and improve the effectiveness of promotion are characteristics of a concentrated growth strategy. High success rates of new products also are tied to avoiding situations that require undeveloped skills, such as serving new customers and markets, acquiring new technologies, building new channels, developing new promotional abilities, and facing new competition.

Specific conditions in the corporation's environment are favorable to concentrated growth: (1) The industry is resistant to major technological advancements. This is usually the case in the late growth and maturity stages of the product life cycle and in product markets where product demand is stable and industry barriers, such as capitalization, are high. (2) Targeted markets are not product saturated. Markets with competitive gaps leave the firm with alternatives for growth, other than taking market share away from competitors. (3) The product market is sufficiently distinctive to dissuade competitors from trying to invade the segment. (4) Necessary inputs are stable in price and quantity and are available in the amounts and at the times needed.

Vertical and Horizontal Integration

If a corporation's current lines of business show real growth potential, it makes sense to maximize resource allocations to existing opportunities. Two avenues for growth—*vertical* and *horizontal*—are available.

Vertical integration is undertaken to increase a corporation's vertical participation in an industry's value chain. It is valuable if the corporation possesses a business unit that has a strong competitive position in a highly attractive industry—especially when the industry's technology is predictable and markets are growing rapidly. Although *backward integration* is usually more profitable than *forward integration,* such moves often involve an expensive investment in assets. Additionally vertical integration can reduce a corporation's strategic flexibility by creating an exit barrier that prevents the company from leaving the industry if its fortunes decline.

Horizontal growth involves increasing the range of products and services offered to current markets or expanding the firm's presence into a wider number of geographic locations. KLM's decision to purchase a controlling interest in Northwest Airlines, for example, was primarily made to obtain access to American and Asian markets. In recent years, *strategic alliances* have become an increasingly popular way to implement horizontal growth strategies.

Diversification Strategies

The word *diversification* has an extensive variety of applications in connection with many aspects of business activity. We talk about diversifying into new industries, technologies, supplier bases, customer segments, geographical regions, or sources of funds. However, in a strategic context, the appropriate use of the term involves product-market diversification—the strategy of investing corporate resources in a number of different product/market combinations.

The long-term success of Philip Morris is based to a great extent on diversification. The company is a leader in three major consumer goods: tobacco, food, and beer. Its tobacco business sells under the popular brands of Marlboro, Parliament, and Virginia Slims. Philip Morris's cigarette business leads the U.S. market with a 50.5 percent market share and is the global leader in tobacco. Its food business, Kraft Foods, sells products under the brands of Oscar Mayer, Maxwell House, Post, and Nabisco. Globally, Kraft Foods is the second-largest food company. Miller Brewing is Philip Morris's third major business segment.

Philip Morris's diversified strategy is notable for two main reasons. First, the company has a risk-averse attitude. With a beta of 0.24, the corporation's stock price volatility relative to that of the average in its businesses is extremely low. Second, Philip Morris's businesses are noncyclical. The corporation's operating revenues have steadily increased over the past ten years. In 1991, the revenues were $56 million, and they increased every year thereafter to $80 million in 2000. This ten-year span included both recessionary and inflationary periods in the United States and overseas.[2]

The adoption of a diversification strategy poses a great challenge to corporate executives. Whereas some corporations such as General Electric, Disney, and 3M have been very successful in diversifying their interests, failures such as Quaker Oats (with Snapple) and RCA (with computers, carpets, and rental cars) are reminders that diversifications are fraught with risk.

Internal and external inducements to growth are primary drivers for diversification. Internal inducements originate from the corporation's current competitive position and include such influences as the need to counterbalance cyclical performance and the opportunity to use excess capacity. External inducements are conditions in a firm's external environment that draw it into new businesses. They can take the forms of opportunities—leveraging a strong brand name, for example—or of threats as in the case of declining demand in key segments.

Constantinos Markides suggests that senior executives ask themselves six critical questions to evaluate the risks associated with a diversification strategy:[3]

1. *What can our company do better than any of its competitors in its current markets?* This question is aimed at identifying a company's unique strategic assets. It forces the organization to think about how it can add value to an acquired company or in a new market.

2. *What strategic assets are needed to succeed in the new market?* Having *some* of the skills needed to successfully stake out a position in a new market is not enough. A company must have, or know where to get, *all* of them.

3. *Can the firm catch or leapfrog competitors?* If a company does not have all of the requisite skills to succeed in a new market, it must know how to buy them, develop them, or make them unnecessary by changing the rules of competition. When Canon diversified from cameras into photocopiers, it lacked a strong direct sales force capable of challenging Xerox in its customer base of large companies. Rather than investing in a sales force, Canon decided to target small and midsize companies as well as the consumer market through established dealers.

4. *Will diversification break up strategic assets that need to be kept together?* Corporate assets are often synergistic. Cannibalizing one or more carefully developed assets from an integrated set developed for one product market for use in a new competitive arena can destroy the profit-generating synergies of the parent firm.

5. *Will our firm simply be a player in the new market or will it be a winner?*

6. *What can the corporation learn by diversifying, and are we organized to learn it?*

Answering these questions can reduce uncertainty. However, it is clear that diversification is not a panacea for rescuing corporations with mediocre performance. It can improve shareholder value, but diversification needs to be planned carefully in the context of an overall corporate strategy.

Mergers and Acquisitions

Companies can implement diversification strategies through internal development, cooperative ventures such as alliances, or mergers and acquisitions. Internal development can be slow and expensive. Alliances involve all of the complications and compromises of a renegotiable relationship, including debates over investments and profits.

As a result, permanently bonding with another company is sometimes seen as the easiest way to diversify. Two terms describe such relationships: *mergers* and *acquisitions*. A merger signifies that two companies have joined to form one company. An acquisition occurs when one firm buys another. To outsiders, the difference might appear small and related less to ownership control than to financing. However, the critical difference is often in management control. In acquisitions, the management team of the buyer tends to dominate decisions of the combined company.

SCP Pool Corp., the largest independent distributor of swimming-pool supplies in the United States, has implemented a successful acquisition strategy to improve its margins and gain market share in a highly fragmented industry.[4] SCP distributes 60,000 national brand and private-label products to 40,000 customers, including pool remodelers and builders, independent retail stores, and pool-repair and service companies. As of 2002, SCP operated 173 service centers in North America and Europe. The company's growth since 1997 has been led by 12 acquisitions.

The number of swimming pools in individual residents has grown steadily over the past 10 years, mirroring demographic trends. The average age of a swimming pool owner is 47, so the industry grew with the aging of baby boomers. In 2002, 83 million Americans were 45–74-year olds, compared to 67 million in 1995. The pool industry also benefited from the rapid growth of the U.S. Sunbelt region where SCP has a high concentration of service centers.

SCP competes mainly against small distributors. The top four distributors including SCP control 50 percent of the U.S. market, while 170 local and regional distributors control the other half. SCP achieves economies of scale through its acquisitions as shown in its steadily improving return on capital. Its margins have widened substantially as it's increasing size gives SCP added leverage over suppliers and pricing strength with customers. It also has a competitive advantage over smaller players due to the greater breadth products it offers and a higher level of service.

The advantages of buying an existing player can be compelling. An acquisition can quickly position a firm in a new business or market. It also eliminates a potential competitor and therefore does not contribute to the development of excess capacity.

Acquisitions, however, are also generally expensive. Premiums of 30 percent or more over the current value of the stock are not uncommon. This means that, although sellers often pocket handsome profits, acquiring companies frequently lose shareholder value. The process by which merger-and-acquisition decisions are made contributes to this problem. In theory, acquisitions are part of a corporate diversification strategy based on the explicit identification of the most suitable players in the most attractive industries as targets to be purchased. Acquisition strategies should also specify a comprehensive framework for the due diligence assessments of targets, plans for integrating acquired companies into the corporate portfolio, and a careful determination of how much is too much to pay.

In practice, the acquisition process is far more complex. Once the board has approved plans to expand into new businesses or markets, or once a potential target company has been identified, the time to act is typically short. The ensuing pressures to "do a deal" are intense—emanating from senior executives, directors, investment bankers who stand to gain from *any* deal, shareholder groups, and competitors bidding against the firm. The environment can become frenzied. Valuations tend to rise as corporations become overconfident in their ability to add value to the target company and as expectations regarding synergies reach new heights. Due diligence is conducted more quickly than is desirable and tends to be confined to financial considerations. Integration planning takes a back seat. Differences in corporate cultures are discounted. In this climate, even the best-designed strategies can fail to produce a successful outcome, as many companies and their shareholders have learned.

What can be done to increase the effectiveness of the merger-and-acquisition process? Although there are no formulas for success, six themes have emerged:

1. Successful acquisitions are usually part of a well-developed corporate strategy.
2. Diversification through acquisition is an ongoing, long-term process that requires patience.
3. Successful acquisitions usually result from disciplined strategic analysis, which looks at industries first before it targets companies, while recognizing that good deals are firm-specific.
4. There are only a few ways by which an acquirer can add value, and before proceeding with an acquisition, the buying company should be able to specify how synergies will be achieved and value created.
5. Objectivity is essential even though it is hard to maintain once the acquisition chase ensues.
6. Most acquisitions flounder on implementation—strategies for implementation should be formulated before the acquisition is completed and executed quickly after the acquisition deal is closed.

Cooperative Strategies

Cooperative strategies—joint ventures, strategic alliances, and other partnering arrangements—have become more important in recent years. For many corporations, cooperative strategies capture the benefits of internal development and acquisition while avoiding the drawbacks of both.

Globalization is an important factor in the rise of cooperative ventures. In a global competitive environment, going it alone often means taking extraordinary risks. Escalating fixed costs associated with achieving global market coverage, keeping up with the latest technology, and increased exposure to currency and political risk all make risk-sharing a necessity in many industries. For many companies, a global strategic posture without alliances would be untenable.

Cooperative strategies take many forms and are forged for many different reasons. However, the fundamental motivation in every case is that the corporation is able to spread its investments over a range of options, each with a different risk profile. Essentially, the corporation is trading off the likelihood of a major payoff against the ability to optimize its investments by betting on multiple options. The key drivers that attract executives to cooperative strategies include the need for risk-sharing, the corporation's funding limitations, and the desire to gain market and technology access.[5]

Risk Sharing

Many companies cannot afford "bet the company" moves to participate in all product markets of strategic interest. Whether a corporation is considering entry into a global market or investments in new technologies, the dominant logic dictates that companies prioritize their strategic interests and balance them according to risk.

Funding Limitations

Commonly, a company focused on building sustainable advantage by establishing dominance in *all* of the business's value-creating activities. Through cumulative investment and vertical integration, a corporation built barriers to entry that were hard to penetrate. However, as the globalization of the business environment accelerates and the technology race intensifies, such a strategic posture becomes increasingly difficult to sustain. Going it alone is no longer practical in many industries. To compete in the global arena, companies must incur immense fixed costs with a shorter payback period and at a higher level of risk.

Market Access

Companies usually recognize their lack of prerequisite knowledge, infrastructure, or critical relationships necessary for the distribution of their products to new customers. Cooperative strategies can help them fill the gaps. For example, Hitachi has an alliance with Deere & Company in North America and with Fiat Allis in Europe to distribute its hydraulic excavators. This arrangement makes sense because Hitachi's product line is too narrow to justify a separate distribution network. What is more, customers benefit because the gaps in its product line are filled with quality products such as bulldozers and wheel loaders from its alliance partners.

Technology Access

A large number of products rely on so many different technologies that few companies can afford to remain at the forefront of all of them. Carmakers increasingly rely on advances in electronics, application software developers depend on new features delivered by Microsoft in its next-generation operating platform, and advertising agencies need more and more sophisticated tracking data to formulate schedules for clients. At the same time, the pace at which technology is spreading globally is increasing, making time an even more critical variable in developing and sustaining competitive advantage. It is usually beyond the capabilities, resources, and good luck in R&D of any corporation to garner the technological advantage needed to independently create disruption in the marketplace. Therefore, partnering with technologically compatible companies to achieve the requisite level of excellence is often essential. The implementation of such strategies, in turn, increases the speed at which technology diffuses around the world.

Other reasons to pursue a cooperative strategy are a lack of particular *management skills,* an *inability to add value in-house,* and a *lack of acquisition opportunities* because of size, geographical, or ownership restrictions. The relevance of particular drivers varies by industry and by company within an industry (Figure 7-1).

Cooperative strategies cover a wide spectrum of nonequity, cross-equity, and shared-equity arrangements. Selecting the most appropriate arrangement involves analyzing the nature of the opportunity, the mutual strategic interests in the cooperative venture, and prior experience with joint ventures of both partners. The essential question is: How can we structure this opportunity to maximize the benefit(s) to both parties?

The airline industry provides a good example of some drivers and issues involved in forging strategic alliances. Although the U.S. industry has been deregulated for some time, international aviation remains controlled by a host of bilateral agreements that smack of protectionism. Outdated limits on foreign ownership further distort natural market forces toward a more-global industry posture. As a consequence, airline

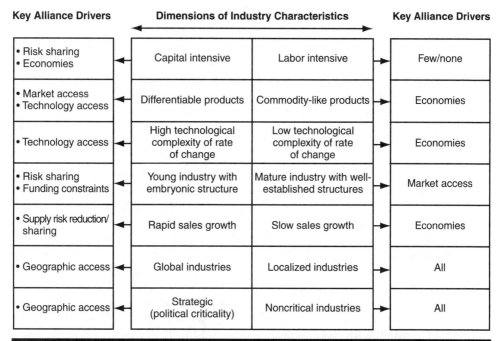

Key Alliance Drivers	Dimensions of Industry Characteristics		Key Alliance Drivers
• Risk sharing • Economies	Capital intensive	Labor intensive	Few/none
• Market access • Technology access	Differentiable products	Commodity-like products	Economies
• Technology access	High technological complexity of rate of change	Low technological complexity of rate of change	Economies
• Risk sharing • Funding constraints	Young industry with embryonic structure	Mature industry with well-established structures	Market access
• Supply risk reduction/ sharing	Rapid sales growth	Slow sales growth	Economies
• Geographic access	Global industries	Localized industries	All
• Geographic access	Strategic (political criticality)	Noncritical industries	All

FIGURE 7-1   Drivers of Cooperative Strategy

Reprinted with permission from Booz Allen Hamilton. Copyright 1993. www.boozallen.com

companies have been forced to confront the challenges of global competition in other ways. With takeovers and mergers blocked, they have formed all kinds of alliances—from code sharing to aircraft maintenance to frequent flyer plans.

It is widely expected that four major groups will dominate the airline industry before long. The Oneworld alliance includes British Airways, American Airlines, Qantas, Canadian Airways, and Cathay Pacific. The Star alliance is led by United Airlines and Lufthansa and includes a number of smaller carriers including Thai, SAS, Air Canada, Varig, SAA, Singapore, ANA, ANX, and Ansett. A third group, headed by KLM and Northwest, has signed up Continental and Alitalia. The final group is composed of Delta, Swissair, Sabena, and Austrian Airlines.

The Allianced Enterprise

Strategic alliances are important both because of their popularity and because of their unique effects on corporate structure. In fact, they characterize the revolutionary strategic activity that is ongoing in many industries. Successful alliances can bring about higher growth, higher profitability, and higher market valuations. More than 20 percent of the revenue generated by the top 2000 U.S. and European companies now comes from alliances, and this percentage is expected to climb. Many executives believe that the ability to form successful alliances is a core competency that survivors and thrivers in their industries must master.

Global industries are undergoing rapid structural change, and a new model is being adopted—the Allianced Enterprise. John Harbison, Albert Viscio, Peter Pekar, and David Moloney outline a blueprint for this new model in a report sponsored by Booz-Allen & Hamilton.[6] Their report describes the various alliance opportunities that are created in different phases of the business life cycle.

According to the Booz-Allen team, each business life cycle phase is a key driver of alliance imperatives. As shown in Figure 7-2, product innovation, credibility, and access to capital are the key drivers of alliance initiatives in the early growth stage. The alliance's external value and market and customer reach are the most important factors in both the rapid growth and consolidation phases. In the stability stage, reduced cost, value-chain strengthening, and product extension become the most important factors.

Microsoft is a company that uses the Allianced Enterprise model. The software giant had a market capitalization of $600 million at the time of its IPO in 1986, which it increased to over $500 billion in market capitalization by 2000. Alliances played a critical role in this growth. The company's first major partnership was with IBM to develop DOS. This alliance was followed by its "Wintel" alliance with Intel that helped Microsoft emerge as the dominant leader in the operating systems market. Microsoft continues to search for strategic partners. In 1999 and 2000, the company announced two alliances per day on average.

Business life cycle phases are the driving forces influencing strategic alliance decisions. A series of steps called *forcing techniques* can be used to locate alliance opportunities across the life cycle phases. Figure 7-3 illustrates a forcing technique. It was

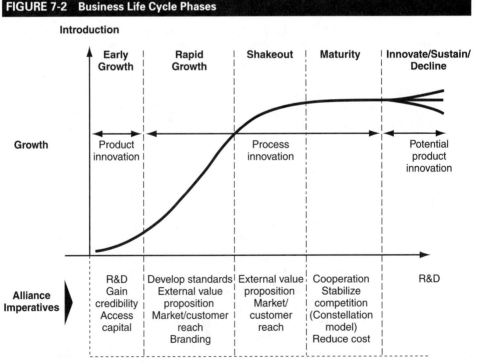

FIGURE 7-2   Business Life Cycle Phases

Source: Adapted from Booz-Allen & Hamilton

Examples

LIFE CYCLE EVENT ANALYSIS—INDIVIDUAL INVESTMENT LIFE CYCLE

	Acquire funds to invest	Identify investment needs	Investigate available products	Effect transaction	Monitor investment performance	Manage tax	Sell investment
Potential Partners for a Retail Funds Manager	• Financial institutions without investment offerings (e.g., credit unions, small banks) • Employers • Professional associations/ affinity groups • Real estate agents • HR consultants	• Accountants • Independent financial advisers • Investment magazines • Investment clubs • Financial planning software • Financial planning Internet sites	• Independent financial advisers • Investment magazines • Investment clubs • Investment Internet sites	• Stockbrokers • Credit unions/small banks • Financial management software (e.g., Quicken, MS Money) • Utilities • Credit card companies	• Investment magazines/ finance papers • Financial management software (e.g., Quicken, MS Money) • Investment tracking Internet sites	• Accountants • Tax return preparation agents	• Independent financial advisers • Stockbrokers

FIGURE 7-3   Forcing Techniques to Surface Alliance Options

Source: Booz-Allen & Hamilton

designed by the management team of a retail funds company that was trying to identify partnership opportunities that would increase its distribution.

Approximately 10,000 strategic alliances are formed worldwide each year. These partnerships are an interrelated web of activities designed to gain competitive advantage. The increasing number of alliances is creating challenges for managers, and is leading to changes in the way that firms are organized. The traditional *command and control* model is not sufficiently effective for managing the complex set of relationships among multiple business partners created by strategic alliances. Companies require more flexible and dynamic models to reflect the market environment and partnership structures.

Four new models are emerging to guide companies with multiple strategic alliances: franchise, portfolio, cooperative, and constellation. These models are shown in Figure 7-4.

When gaps in an organization's value chain are greater than any one partner can fill, managers can turn to the *franchise* model. In this model, a company develops an alliance structure that can be easily replicated for a class of partnerships. Nintendo uses the franchise model to fill in a key capability need—the development of games for its consoles.

The *portfolio* model, also known as *hub-and-spoke,* involves the establishment of multiple alliances managed as a single portfolio. One company acts as the hub for the alliances and manages the external partners. AT&T and Time Warner each use this approach.

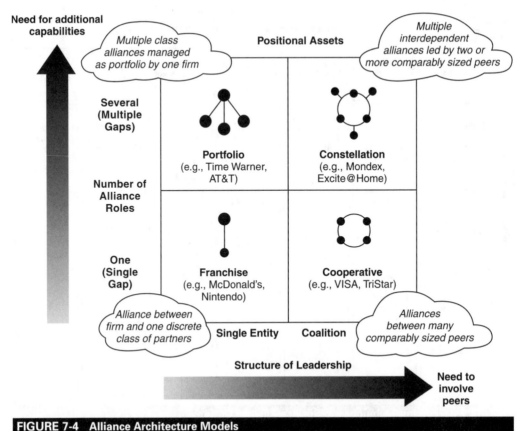

FIGURE 7-4 Alliance Architecture Models

Source: Booz-Allen & Hamilton

With the *cooperative* model, the alliance is at the center. Customer relationships shift from individual company members to the alliance center. No one company is in control; instead all partners work together toward the same unifying goal. Tri-Star—an alliance among CBS, Columbia Pictures, and HBO—is an example of the cooperative model.

Companies that utilize the *constellation* model develop breakout strategies designed to put competitors on the defensive. A constellation requires its own center, one that is focused on creating value for the extended entity in the areas of strategic leadership, capability brokering, identity, control, and capital. For example, entering the e-procurement industry requires a considerable number of partners that can play multiple alliance roles, which the design of an alliance constellation can facilitate.

DISINVESTMENT STRATEGIES: SELL-OFFS, SPIN-OFFS, AND LIQUIDATIONS

At times, management is faced with the prospect of having to retrench in one or more of its lines of business. To sell off an SBU to a competitor or to spin it off into a separate company makes sense when analysis confirms the corporation is the wrong corporate parent for the business. In such circumstances, value can be realized by giving the markets the opportunity to decide the fate of the business. If there are no potential buyers, liquidation may have to be considered.

Unilever P.L.C. is a British-Dutch consumer products company whose brands include Lipton teas, Ragu sauces, WishBone salad dressing, and Wisk detergent. In 1999, Unilever announced a Path to Growth program that involved focusing on fewer, stronger brands to promote faster growth. The plan guided Unilever in streamlining its brand portfolio from 1600 brands to 400 well-known brands. As a part of the program, Unilever began aggressively buying high-growth brands from other companies. In addition, the Path to Growth strategy specified that underperforming or mismatched brands would be reorganized or divested.

The acquisition of the Bestfoods Company by Unilever illustrates this strategy. Through this acquisition, Unilever acquired Hellman's mayonnaise, Knorrs soup and sauces, and Skippy peanut butter. Part two of the plan involved divesting the Bestfoods Baking Unit, a division of the Bestfoods acquisition. Bestfoods Baking was a leading fresh baked goods company in the United States providing popular products like Entenmann's sweet baked goods and Thomas's English muffins, bagels, and waffles. Bestfoods Baking had great profit potential, but did not fit Unilever's strategic goal of focusing on few high-growth brands. Therefore, the Bestfoods Baking divestiture positioned Unilever closer to its strategic goals and rewarded it with sizable proceeds of $1.77 billion from the 2001 sale of the unit to Canada's George Weston Ltd.[7] These examples show that, at times, sell-offs, spin-offs, and liquidations are key components of carefully formulated strategies designed to optimize profit potential through disinvestment strategies.

MANAGEMENT STYLE OPTIONS: THE ROLE OF THE CORPORATE OFFICE

Outcome or Behavior Control?

Management style addresses the third side of the triangle in the resource-based approach to corporate strategy—the organizational structure, systems, and processes that are used to implement corporate strategy. It deals with such questions as: What are the roles of corporate executives in shaping and executing divisional strategies? How do they control the activities of the various semiautonomous business units? How do they provide coherence to the various corporate activities as a whole?

Corporations differ in important ways in how they organize and implement their decision-making. Some, like Textron or ABB, operate with a small headquarters staff, give substantial autonomy to their operating units, and exercise control primarily by setting financial standards of performance. They focus primarily on *outcome control*. Others, such as Cooper Industries, take a much more active role in running divisional operations, and effectively exercise *behavior control* by getting involved in how-to decisions.

Most companies employ a mixture of the two positions. For example, in many corporations, executives base their divisional performance evaluations primarily on financial measures (outcome control), but are more involved in initiatives such as upgrading manufacturing processes or implementing total quality programs (behavior control).

Outcome control is typically more appropriate when a single measure of current financial performance, such as cash flow, is appropriate to assess a unit's strategic position;

when factors outside the business unit have only a minor effect on performance; and when there is little need for coordination between the various business units. For these reasons, outcome control is typically more relevant to companies with a portfolio of unrelated businesses, whereas parenting styles involving substantial behavior control are more likely to be found in companies made up of related businesses.

EVALUATING STRATEGY OPTIONS AT THE CORPORATE LEVEL

A large number of potentially viable strategy options are typically offered at the corporate level. The sheer number and enormous diversity of the alternatives complicate the determination of the best option. Is internal growth better than external growth? Is concentrated growth preferable to diversification? Are cooperative strategies the answer? How do these options affect our parenting strategies? Clearly, not all options can be equally well managed. In fact, as history has shown, many strategy options are likely to fail, because of flaws either in the strategic fit or in implementation.

Issues of Valuation

The evaluation of strategic options always has a quantitative component. Every major strategic decision involves a cost-benefit calculation, whether formal or informal, precise or approximate. Whether the issue is opening a new factory overseas, entering a strategic partnership or restructuring the portfolio, how a company values its strategic alternatives is crucially important to how its corporate strategy evolves. What is more, as senior executives find themselves under increased pressure for performance and accountability by shareholders and other stakeholders, they are asked to share not only what decisions they have made but also how they arrived at their conclusions. As a consequence, valuation has become an increasingly important skill in developing and executing a corporate strategy.

Many companies use a mix of approaches to deal with the issue of valuation. Some are formal, based on analytic models and financial theories; others are informal, often representing little more than ad hoc heuristics and traditional industry guidelines. Aspects of valuation are sometimes done explicitly; others are done implicitly. The methods and concepts used reflect the far-ranging skills, attitudes, and experiences of the executives who apply them.

With the push for greater accountability and better performance, a trend toward more formal, explicit, and institutionalized valuation of strategic options has emerged. Terms such as shareholder value analysis (SVA), discounted cash flow (DCF) analysis, and economic value added (EVA) are heard with greater frequency at board meetings, shareholder gatherings, and briefings to analysts. The greater emphasis on formal evaluation is laudable; it brings a much-needed rigor to the task of strategy assessment at the corporate level. The implementation of such advanced valuation methods, however, presents a host of challenges.

Techniques

The complexity of putting a numerical value on a corporate strategy is daunting. The simple fact is, many popular press accounts not withstanding, that there is no single, fully developed financial theory that can produce unambiguous estimates of value in dynamic strategic environments. Techniques such as *discounted cash flow analysis* are helpful in valuing well-defined, relatively predictable alternatives for which reasonably accurate cash flow forecasts can be generated. However, valuing strategic alternatives in situations characterized by higher levels of uncertainty is another matter entirely.

Timothy Luehrman distinguishes among three classes of valuation problems. Valuing *operations* is the most common valuation issue. It involves putting a value on an ongoing business or deciding on a specific strategic investment. Here discounted cash flow methods can be used.[8] Valuing *opportunities*—the second type of valuation problem—is akin to valuing options rather than an underlying stock. It places a value on possible future operations. Deciding on how much to spend on R&D and on what kind is an example; such a decision foreshadows future alternatives. Here *option pricing* methods are more appropriate than discounted cash flow schemes, although their application is far from straightforward. Finally, valuing *ownership claims*—important in assessing such strategic options as joint ventures and alliances—involves assessing the value of the venture as well as the equity cash flows associated with it. *Equity cash flow analysis* is the preferred technique under this scenario.

Deciding on an overall, theoretically consistent, quantitative methodology for evaluating a complex corporate strategy proposal involving multiple options is not a simple undertaking. Even though progress has been made with user-friendly computer models, specialized skills will always be needed to successfully implement these techniques.

Finally, valuation has a subjective element. It is considered last because it is most important. Quantitative analysis provides the underpinning for executive forecasting. It narrows the executives' field of vision so that their conceptual powers can be focused on the most promising options. To the extent that the future behaviors of customers, competitors, and other stakeholders are best predicted by their past behaviors, executives with relevant experience are best prepared to help the corporation see "around the corner," as all strategy formulation requires.

Developing a corporate strategy is one of the most challenging tasks facing senior executives. While the body of knowledge about what works and what does not work grows daily, most issues remain unresolved. What is more, the rapid changes that are taking place in the global competitive environment will soon make much of today's knowledge obsolete. As a result, formulating effective corporate strategies will always require more than a combination of in-depth quantitative analysis. It will demand keen managerial insight, intuition, and creativity.

Notes

1. J. A. Pearce II and J. W. Harvey, "Concentrated Growth Strategies," *Academy of Management Executive,* February 1990, pp. 61–68.

2. A. Hughes, "Why Philip Morris' Shares Are Smokin'," *Business Week,* December 27, 2000; R. Joy, "Big Gains For Big Mo," *Business Week,* February 12, 2001.

3. C. C. Markides, "To Diversify or Not To Diversify?" *Harvard Business Review,* November–December 1997, pp. 93–99.

4. M. Kaminis, "A Stock Worth Diving Into," *Business Week,* March 14, 2002.

5. "A Practical Guide to Alliances: Leapfrogging the Learning Curve," Los Angeles: Booz-Allen & Hamilton, 1993.

6. This section is based on J. R. Harbison, A. Viscio, P. Pekar, Jr., and D. Moloney, "The Allianced Enterprise: Breakout Strategy for the New Millennium," Los Angeles: Booz-Allen & Hamilton, Inc., 2000.

7. A. Cowell, 2000. "Unilever Says Purchase Fits Into Growth Strategy," *New York Times,* June 7, 2000, p. C8; C. L. Hays, "Unilever Deal for Bestfoods Signals More Acquisitions," *New York Times,* June 7, 2000, pp. C1, C8.

8. T. A. Luehrman, "What's it Worth? A General Manager's Guide to Valuation," *Harvard Business Review,* May–June 1997, pp. 132–142. Luehrman recommends replacing traditional *discounted cash flow analysis using the weighted-average cost of capital* with the *adjusted present value approach* to facilitate adjustments for items such as tax shields and changes in capital structure.

Formulating
a Global Strategy

INTRODUCTION

The globalization of the competitive landscape has forced many companies to fundamentally rethink their strategies. Whereas once only a few industries such as oil could be labeled truly global, today many—from pharmaceuticals to aircraft to computers—are becoming global in scale and scope. As a consequence, creating a global competitive advantage has become a key strategic issue for many companies.

Global strategy formulation requires making decisions about which strategy elements can and should be globalized and to what extent. Key questions for analysis include: (1) What markets and/or regions should a company compete in and why? (2) To what degree can and should products and services be standardized? (3) Is it advantageous to adopt a more or less uniform market positioning worldwide? (4) What value-added activities should it keep in-house, outsource, or relocate for competitive advantage? and (5) How can competitive responses be most effectively coordinated on a global basis? Answers to these questions help define a company's global strategic focus on a continuum from a truly global orientation to a more local one.

To create a global vision, a company must carefully define what globalization means for its particular business. This greatly depends on the industry, the product or service, and the requirements for global success. For Coca-Cola, it meant duplicating a substantial part of its value-creation process—from product formulation to marketing and delivery—throughout the world. For Intel, creating global competitive advantage is based on attaining technological leadership and preferred component supplier status on a global basis. For a midsize company, it may mean setting up a host of small foreign subsidiaries and forging numerous alliances. For still others, it may mean something entirely different. Thus, while it is tempting to think of global strategy in universal terms, globalization is a highly company- and industry-specific issue. It forces a company to rethink its strategic intent, global architecture, core competencies, and entire current product and service mix. For many companies the outcome demands dramatic changes in the way they do business—with whom, how, and why.

This chapter is divided into five sections. First, we identify the main drivers behind industry and market globalization. Next, we present a generic characterization of global strategic postures. In the third section, we look at global strategy formulation by analyzing its principal dimensions. In the fourth and fifth sections we discuss two special topics: entry strategies and global strategic risk.

INDUSTRY AND MARKET GLOBALIZATION

Globalization: A Work in Progress

The words *global economy* should be used with great care. Trade and foreign investment among and within the so-called Triad countries—the United States, the European Union, and Japan—still account for the bulk of global economic activity, and more than four-fifths of the world's 500 largest publicly traded companies still are headquartered in the Triad.[1] The formation of *regional trading blocks*—stepping stones to free trade on a global basis—has been instrumental in defining the path of economic globalization. Together, they account for almost 60 percent of world trade.

The European Union (EU), with 15 countries, has grown to account for almost a quarter of all the world's trade. The North American Free Trade Agreement (NAFTA) currently only has three members—Canada, the United States, and Mexico—but accounts for nearly 8 percent of world trade. The Association of South East Asian Nations (ASEAN) coordinates trade policies and promotes economic cooperation in southeast Asia. EUROMED is a group of 12 Mediterranean countries that have agreed to establish a free-trade zone by 2010. An organization called Asia Pacific Economic Cooperation (APEC), which consists of 18 countries around the Pacific Rim, hopes to create free trade and investment in the region by 2010 for its higher-income members, and by 2020 for the rest. Finally, Mercosur is a small trading club, representing 0.3 percent of world trade, with Argentina, Brazil, Paraguay, and Uruguay as members.

The globalization of the world economy, therefore, is very much a work in progress. Its progress, however, is unmistakable. *Economic* globalization has been joined by *political* globalization. In the aftermath of the collapse of communism in 1989, many countries opted for democracy and market-driven economies. As a consequence, trade and cross-country investment increased, and deregulation and privatization flourished. *Technological* globalization accelerated this rapid diffusion of free enterprise. Together, economic, political, and technological globalization have spawned a new phenomenon: *psychological* globalization, defined as the gradual convergence of human expectations on a global scale.

As needs and preferences continue to converge globally, customers in different parts of the world will increasingly demand similar products and levels of service—from cars to PCs to entertainment. This creates opportunities for scale advantages through the marketing of more or less standardized offerings. How much needs, tastes, and preferences will converge will vary greatly by product and industry, and depends on such factors as the importance of cultural variables, disposable incomes, and the degree of homogeneity in the conditions in which the product is consumed or used.

Industry Globalization Drivers

George Yip has identified four sets of *industry globalization drivers*—underlying conditions that create the potential for an industry to become more global and, as a consequence, for the potential viability of a global approach to strategy (Figure 8-1).[2] *Market drivers* are measures that define how customer behavior patterns evolve, and how their needs converge around the world. They are important because they indicate whether worldwide channels of distribution can develop, marketing platforms are transferable, and lead countries can be identified in which most innovation takes

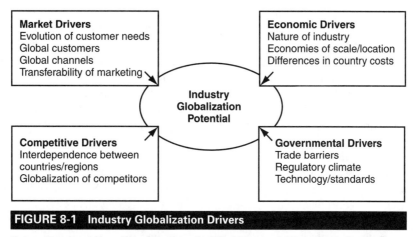

FIGURE 8-1   Industry Globalization Drivers

Source: Reprinted from *Columbia Journal of World Business,* Winter 1988, George S. Yip, Pierre M. Loene, and Michael E. Yoshino, "How to Take Your Company to the Global Market," pp. 14–26, copyright © 1988, with permission from Elsevier Science.

place. *Cost globalization* drivers are factors that define the opportunity for global scale or scope economics, experience effects, sourcing efficiencies reflecting differentials in costs between countries or regions, and technology advantages. They shape the economics of an industry. *Competitive* drivers are defined by the actions of competing firms—the extent to which competitors from different continents enter the fray, globalize their strategies and corporate capabilities, and create interdependence between geographical markets. *Government* drivers include such factors as favorable trade policies, a benign regulatory climate, and common product and technology standards.

Market Drivers

There are many forces pushing companies to think more globally, including meeting foreign competition head on, better serving an increasingly global customer base, exploiting diverse capabilities and cost advantages, and taking advantage of an easing global regulatory environment. *Meeting changing customer expectations,* however, is the primary reason many companies need to strengthen their global posture.

A high degree of regional or global similarity in product or service requirements and features calls for a *global product or service strategy*—implying substantial standardization. Marriott offers similar, but not identical, services around the world. Kentucky Fried Chicken, while adapting to local tastes and preferences, has standardized many elements of its operations. Software, oil products, and accounting services also increasingly look alike no matter where they are purchased.

In many countries, regulations require considerable local adaptation of products and services; insurance and financial services are illustrations. In such circumstances, similarity might be limited to benefits sought, and therefore a *global benefit strategy* would be more appropriate. When similarities are only confined to the underlying need for the product or service, such as for different types of medical equipment, the strategic focus should be on developing a *global product or service category.*[3]

As consumption patterns become more homogeneous around the world, global branding and marketing will become increasingly important to global success. Global distribution and e-procurement channels are emerging in many industries, causing a further convergence of needs. For some products purchase behavior is still primarily *local;* for others more *regional* procurement patterns have evolved, while *global* sourcing—selecting the best offer from anywhere around the world—is becoming the norm in a growing number of industries. General Electric sources from around the world for all of its businesses. Such global purchasing patterns can take different forms. Sometimes buyers merely seek global price transparency. At other times they desire supporting global logistics, purchasing agreements, or even account management.[4]

Cost Drivers

In a growing number of industries the minimum volume required for cost efficiency is simply no longer available in a single country or region. The pharmaceutical industry provides a good example. The development of many new drugs can no longer be justified on the basis of the economic returns from a single country. As a consequence, economies of scale and scope; experience effects; and exploiting differences in factor costs for product development, manufacturing, and sourcing in different parts of the world have become critical to global success. This can create the need for *critical mass* in different parts of the value chain. For pharmaceutical companies, critical mass in R&D is key to nurturing a strong pipeline of new drugs and compounds; in the airline industry, logistics is a key scale variable; and for soft drinks, market presence and global branding are key to creating global critical mass. Determining which parts of the value chain require critical mass also assists in assessing the need for mergers and acquisitions, and guides the development of key alliances.

Competitive Drivers

The globalization potential of an industry is also influenced by competitive drivers, such as (1) the degree to which total industry sales are made up by export or import volume, (2) the diversity of competitors in terms of their national origin, and (3) the extent to which major players have globalized their operations and created an interdependence between their competitive strategies in different parts of the world. High levels of trade, competitive diversity, and interdependence tend to increase competition and the potential for industry globalization.

An analysis of global competitive drivers should focus on whether competition is primarily waged at the local level or the regional level, or whether it has evolved into a coordinated global pattern. Useful questions to ask include: How many competitive arenas does our company compete in? Do we mainly face the same principal competitors in different parts of the world? Do competitors employ similar strategies in the different arenas? and How necessary is it to coordinate competitive responses on a global scale?

Government Drivers

Some industries are more regulated than others. In the steel industry, for example, the presence or absence of favorable trade policies, technical standards, policies and regulations, and government-operated or -subsidized competitors or customers has a direct influence on a company's global strategic options. In the past, multinationals almost exclusively relied on governments to negotiate the rules of global competition. However, as the politics and economics of global competition have become more closely intertwined, companies are paying greater attention to the nonmarket dimensions of their global strategies aimed at shaping the global competitive environment to their advantage. In the telecommunications industry, falling trade barriers and other deregulatory moves have encouraged companies to pursue more global approaches to their business. The threat of protectionism or reregulation in the steel industry, on the other hand, inhibits industry globalization and causes companies to take a less-global approach.

GENERIC GLOBAL STRATEGIES

At a generic level, we can distinguish between *multinational* (or *multidomestic*), *international,* and *global* or *transnational* strategies. As the name suggests, a *multinational* or *multidomestic* approach is applicable when customer needs and industry conditions vary considerably from country to country, and a high degree of localization is required. One of the world's best-known food companies—Nestle—follows this type of strategy. It allows the company to adapt to differences in local taste preferences and distribution structures. Under this approach, most strategic and operating decisions are made at the local level, i.e., they are decentralized to the business unit in each country.

In industries such as electronic appliances or computer chips in which global strategic advantage heavily depends on effectively developing new products in the home market and sequentially diffusing these innovations to foreign markets through affiliate organizations, an *international* strategic posture may be appropriate. The name reflects the importance of managing the international product life cycle through the transfer of technologies to foreign markets. This strategic posture is common in high-technology industries in which exploiting home country innovation is key to global value creation.

A *global* or *transnational* strategic posture is appropriate when some degree of standardization in products and services, in marketing, and in other aspects of strategy is possible. Coca-Cola and McDonald's, for example, have successfully standardized many of their value-creation activities around the world. In contrast, car manufacturers including Ford, General Motors, Toyota, and DaimlerChrysler have found that, although parts of the vehicle production process can be standardized, differences in customer preferences, driving conditions, and related factors mandate a substantial amount of local adaptation. Thus, a *global* or *transnational* strategic posture represents a hybrid approach in which some parts of the value chain are standardized but others are tailored to local demands. The objective of this approach is to achieve global efficiencies while preserving local responsiveness. Implementing such as strategy can be difficult because it relies more on coordination than direct control.[5]

FORMULATING A GLOBAL STRATEGY

Generic characterizations are useful for categorizing different approaches to global strategy formulation. To craft a specific global strategy, five dimensions of global strategy require further analysis: (1) market participation, (2) standardization/positioning, (3) activity concentration, (4) coordination of decision-making, and (5) nonmarket factors. The objective of these assessments is to make thoughtful decisions about which strategy elements can and should be globalized and to what extent.

Market Participation

Few companies can afford to enter all markets open to them. Even the world's largest companies such as General Electric must exercise strategic discipline in choosing the markets they serve. They must weigh the relative advantages of a direct or indirect presence in different regions of the world. For midsize companies the key to gaining global competitive advantage lies in creating a worldwide resource network through alliances with suppliers, customers, and sometimes competitors. A good strategy for one company, however, might have little chance of succeeding for another. Winning strategies are highly selective in terms of market participation, target realistic market share and profit objectives, and balance stretch with current capabilities.

A global view of market opportunities requires a multidimensional perspective. In many industries we can distinguish between *must* markets—markets in which a company must compete in order to realize its global ambitions—and *nice-to-be-in* markets in which participation is desirable but not critical. *Must* markets include those that are critical from a *volume* perspective, markets that define *technological leadership,* and markets in which key *competitive* battles are played out. In the cell phone industry, for example, Motorola looks to Europe as its primary competitive battleground, but it derives much of its technology from Japan and its sales volume from the United States.

Developing a global presence takes time and requires substantial resources. Ideally, the pace of international expansion is dictated by customer demand. Companies have found, however, that it is sometimes necessary to expand ahead of direct opportunity in order to secure a long-term competitive advantage. China provides a good example. As many companies that entered China in anticipation of its membership in the World Trade Organization have found, however, early commitment to a promising market makes earning a satisfactory return on capital invested difficult. As a result, an increasing number of companies, particularly smaller and midsize corporations, favor global expansion strategies that minimize direct investment. Strategic alliances have made vertical or horizontal integration less important to profitability and shareholder value in many industries. Alliances boost contributions to fixed cost while expanding a company's global reach. At the same time, they can be powerful windows on technology, and greatly expand opportunities to create the core competencies needed to effectively compete on a worldwide basis.

Standardization/Positioning

As globalization advances, many companies are seeking opportunities to standardize core products and services. Reducing cost and enhancing quality are primary motivations for standardization. With a few exceptions, the idea of an identical, fully standardized global product is a myth, however.[6] Even though substantial benefits can be achieved by standardizing key product or service components, some components must be customized. Sony, for example, standardizes substantial portions of its consumer electronics products except for the parts that must meet different national electric standards.

Adopting a more global market positioning is another form of standardization. This does not necessarily mean standardizing all elements of the marketing mix or the process by which marketing decisions are made. Rather, by applying a global, cost-benefit approach to formulating marketing strategy, companies seek to balance flexibility with uniformity. Companies such as Nestle, Coca-Cola, Ford, Unilever, IBM, and Disney have found that a more-global marketing approach can derive important benefits. The use of global branding, for example, helps in building brand recognition and enhancing customer preference, and can reduce worldwide marketing costs.

A useful construct for integrating the product/service and positioning dimensions is the *global branding strategy matrix* (Figure 8-2). It identifies four generic global strategies: (1) a *global (marketing) mix* strategy under which both the offer and the message are the same, (2) a *global offer* strategy characterized by an identical offer but different positioning around the world, (3) a *global message* strategy under which the offer might be different in various parts of the world but the message is the same, and (4) a *global change* strategy under which both the offer and the message are adapted to local market circumstances.[7]

Global mix strategies are relatively rare, reflecting the fact that only a few industries are truly global. They apply (1) when a product's usage patterns and brand potential are homogeneous on a global scale, (2) when scale and scope cost advantages substantially outweigh the benefits of partial or full adaptation, and (3) when competitive circumstances are such that a long-term, sustainable advantage can be secured using a standardized approach.

Global offer strategies apply when the same offer can advantageously be positioned differently in different parts of the world. Holiday Inns, for example, are positioned as first-class hotels in some parts of the Far East and in the value category in the United States. There are several reasons for considering a differential positioning in different parts of the world. When fixed costs associated with the offer are high, when key core benefits offered are identical, and when there are natural market boundaries, adapting the message for stronger local advantage is tempting. Although such strategies increase local promotional budgets, they give country managers a degree of flexibility in positioning the product or service for maximum local advantage. The primary disadvantage associated with this type of strategy is that it could be difficult to sustain or even dangerous in the long term as customers become increasingly global in their outlook and confused by the different messages in different parts of the world.

FIGURE 8-2   The Global Branding Matrix

| | **Message** | |
	Standardized	Tailored
Offer Standardized	*Global mix*	*Global offer*
Offer Tailored	*Global message*	*Global change*

Global message strategies use the same message worldwide but allow for local adaptation of the offer. McDonald's, for example, is positioned virtually identically worldwide, but it serves vegetarian food in India and wine in France. The primary motivation behind this type of strategy is the enormous power behind creating a global brand. In industries in which customers increasingly develop similar expectations, aspirations, and values; in which customers are highly mobile; and in which the cost of product or service adaptation is fairly low, leveraging the global brand potential represented by one message worldwide often outweighs the possible disadvantages associated with factors such as higher local R&D costs. As with global offer strategies, however, global message strategies can be risky in the long run; global customers might not find elsewhere what they expect and regularly experience at home. This could lead to confusion or even alienation.

Global change strategies define a best-fit approach and are by far the most common. For most products some form of adaptation of both the offer and the message is necessary. Differences in a product's usage patterns and benefits sought, brand image, competitive structures, distribution channels, and governmental and other regulations all dictate some form of local adaptation. Corporate factors also play a role. Companies that have achieved a global reach through acquisition, for example, often prefer to leverage local brand names, distribution systems, and suppliers rather than embark on a risky global one-size-fits-all approach. As the markets they serve and the company become more global, selective standardization, of the message and/or the offer itself, can become more attractive.

Activity Concentration

To enhance global competitiveness, companies continuously re-examine (1) which parts of the value-creation process they should perform themselves and which to outsource, (2) whether they can eliminate duplicate operations in different parts of the world and reduce the number of manufacturing sites, and (3) whether they can relocate value-added activities to more cost-effective locations. There are many factors to consider in selecting the right level of participation and the location for key value-added activities. Factor conditions, the presence of supporting industrial activity, the nature and location of the demand for the product, and industry rivalry all should be considered. In addition, such issues as tax consequences, the ability to repatriate profits, currency and political risk, the ability to manage and coordinate in different locations, and synergies with other elements of the company's overall strategy should be factored in.

Concentrating value-added activities and rationalizing operations on a global scale to focus on core skills and technologies can be risky. It can create organization and staffing problems, and increase performance risk at a time when the dependence of one unit on others—the company's own or those of its strategic partners—is increased. Many companies, therefore, adopt a cautious, incremental approach to this aspect of globalizing their operations. Several pharmaceutical companies, for example, have focused primarily on concentrating in key locations only those elements of the value chain that are more easily separated from others, such as R&D. Only a few companies have fully globalized all of their value-added activities.

Increasing standardization or concentrating value-added components in key locations does not necessarily preclude being responsive to local demands. The overriding question is: Which parts of the value-creation process should be standardized or concentrated? A major engineering and construction firm, for example, found that less visible parts of its value-creation process—financing large projects among them—could best be handled globally, whereas customer contact-intensive services such as project management and building maintenance were best managed locally. At the same time, the company globalized its entire estimating, project-tracking, and programming services by constructing a state-of-the-art global information network using standardized software worldwide.

Coordination of Decision-Making

Ultimately, the degree to which decision-making—about which markets to participate in, how to allocate resources, and how to compete—is coordinated on a global scale defines the extent to which globalization has been implemented successfully. Many companies have found that integrating and coordinating decision-making on a global scale are at least as important as control. This can take the form of leveraging regional cost differentials, sharing key resources, cross-subsidizing national or regional battles for market share, or pursuing global brand and distribution positions. In the process, companies might have to reorganize their operations and adopt global corporate structures characterized by production and distribution systems in key markets around the world that enable cross-subsidization, competitive retaliation on a global basis, and world-scale volume.[8]

Nonmarket Dimensions of Global Strategy

An essential difference between formulating strategy in a global and a primarily domestic context concerns the relative influence of nonmarket factors on the competitive environment and corporate performance. Increasingly, global corporate success is influenced by *nonmarket* factors that are governed by social, political, and legal arrangements which directly affect the market environment but are primarily determined and intermediated by public institutions. This greater importance of nonmarket considerations in crafting a global strategy reflects the heterogeneity of the emerging global economy. Different countries have different political, economic, and legal systems, and are at different stages of economic development. Cultures as well as educational and skill levels also can vary dramatically. These differences can have profound implications for the rules that shape global competition and, as a consequence, for crafting a global strategy. An effective global strategy addresses both elements; it has market dimensions that seek to create value through economic performance, and nonmarket strategy dimensions aimed at unlocking competitive opportunity. The nonmarket environment is often nation- or region-specific; it is defined by the institutions, the culture, and the organization of political and economic interests in individual countries or regions. Nonmarket elements therefore tend to be less global than the market dimensions of a global strategy.

Dealing effectively with governments is particularly important in *oligopolistic* industries such as telecommunications that are characterized by regulated competition. In these situations nonmarket dimensions of global strategy can be as important as market dimensions. Political involvement might be necessary to create, preserve, or enhance global competitive advantage because government regulations—whether in infant or established industries—are critical to success. As a consequence, strategy in global, regulated industries should be focused as much on shaping the global competitive environment as on capitalizing on the opportunities it offers.

Political competition, characteristic of *fragmented* industries with significant government intervention, also calls for a judicious mix of market- and nonmarket-based strategic thinking. In contrast to regulated competition in which government policy has a direct effect on individual companies, however, government intervention in political competition often pits one country or region of the world against another. This encourages a whole range of cooperative strategies between similarly affected players, and stimulates strategic action at the country-industry level.

ENTRY STRATEGIES

Getting started on the road toward a more global strategic posture poses a set of unique challenges. Should a company first establish an export base or license its products to gain experience in a newly targeted country or region? Or does the potential associated with first-mover status justify a bolder move such as entering an alliance, making an acquisition, or even starting a new subsidiary? Many companies move from exporting to licensing to a higher investment strategy, in effect treating these choices as a learning curve. Figure 8-3 depicts these choices. Each has distinct advantages and disadvantages.

Exporting, while relatively low risk, also entails substantial costs and limited control. Exporters typically have little control over the marketing and distribution of their products, face high transportation charges and possible tariffs, and must pay distributors for a variety of services. What is more, exporting does not give a company first-hand experience in staking out a competitive position abroad, and it makes it difficult to customize products and services to local tastes and preferences.

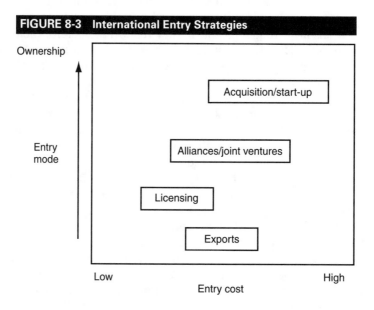

FIGURE 8-3 International Entry Strategies

Licensing reduces cost and also involves limited risk. However, it does not mitigate the substantial disadvantages associated with operating from a distance. As a rule, licensing strategies inhibit control and produce only moderate returns.

Strategic alliances and *joint ventures,* discussed earlier, have become increasingly popular in recent years. They allow companies to share the risks and resources required to enter international markets. And although returns may also have to be shared, they give a company a degree of flexibility not afforded by going it alone through direct investment.

Ultimately, most companies will aim at building their own presence through company-owned facilities in important international markets. *Acquisitions* or *green-field* start-ups represent this ultimate commitment. Acquisition is faster but starting a new, wholly owned subsidiary might be indicated if no suitable acquisition candidates can be found.

Which mode of entry is chosen thus depends on many factors. A learning curve starting with exports, therefore, often makes sense. Licensing can be a helpful step toward a more-substantial local presence. Alliances and joint ventures might allow a company to enter more markets than otherwise would be possible. But to secure a strong local presence, acquisitions or greenfield start-ups might be indicated. In making these decisions, executives should pay particular attention to the degree of risk involved, the subject of the next section.

GLOBAL STRATEGY AND RISK

Even with the best planning, global strategies carry substantial risks. Many globalization strategies represent a considerable stretch of the company's experience base, resources, and capabilities. The firm might target new markets, often in new—for the company— cultural settings. It might seek new technologies, initiate new partnerships, or adopt market share objectives that require earlier or greater commitments than current returns can justify. In the process, new and different forms of competition can be encountered, and it could turn out that the economics model that got the company to its current position is no longer applicable. Often, a more-global posture implies exposure to different cyclical patterns, currency, and political risk. In addition, there are substantial costs associated with coordinating global operations. As a consequence, before deciding to enter a foreign country or continent, companies should carefully analyze the risks involved. Finally, companies should recognize that the management style that proved successful on a domestic scale might turn out to be ineffective in a global setting.

The risks a company can encounter in the international business environment can be of a *political, legal, financial/economic,* or *sociocultural* nature.

Political risk relates to politically induced actions and policies initiated by a foreign government. Its assessment involves an evaluation of the stability of a country's current government and of its relationships with other countries. A high level of risk affects ownership of physical assets and intellectual property, security of personnel, and as a consequence, the potential for trouble. Analysts frequently divide political risk into two subcategories: *global* and *country-specific risk.* Global risk affects all of a company's multinational operations, whereas country-specific risk relates to investments in a specific foreign country. We can distinguish between *macro* and *micro* political risk.

Macro risk is concerned with how foreign investment in general in a particular country is affected. By reviewing the government's past use of *soft* policy instruments such as blacklisting, indirect control of prices, or strikes in particular industries, and *hard* policy tools such as expropriation, confiscation, nationalization, or compulsory local share-holding, a company can be better prepared for potential future government action. At the micro level, risk analysis is focused on a particular company or group of companies. A weak balance sheet, questionable accounting practices, or a regular breach of contracts should give rise to concerns.

Legal risk is risk that multinational companies encounter in the legal arena in a particular country. Legal risk is often closely tied to political country risk. An assessment of legal risk requires analyzing the foundations of a country's legal system and determining whether the laws are properly enforced. Legal risk analysis therefore involves becoming familiar with a country's enforcement agencies and their scope of operation. As many companies have learned, numerous countries have written laws protecting a multinational's rights but rarely enforce them. Entering such countries can expose a company to a host of risks, including the loss of intellectual property, technology, and trademarks.

Financial/economic risk is analogous to operating and financial risk at home. The volatility of a country's macroeconomic performance and the country's ability to meet its financial obligations directly affect performance. A nation's currency competitiveness and fluctuation are important indicators of a country's stability—both financial and political—and its willingness to embrace changes and innovations. In addition, financial risk assessment should consider such factors as how well the economy is being managed, the level of the country's economic development, working conditions, infrastructure, technological innovation, and the availability of natural/human resources.

Societal/cultural risk is the risk associated with operating in a different sociocultural environment. For example, it might be advisable to analyze specific ideologies; the relative importance of ethnic, religious, and nationalistic movements; and the country's ability to cope with changes that will, sooner or later, be induced by foreign investment. Thus, elements such as the standard of living, patriotism, religious factors, or the presence of charismatic leaders can play a huge role in the evaluation of these risks.

NOTES

1. Alan M. Rugman, *The End of Globalization,* Random House Business Books, 2001.

2. This section is based on George S. Yip, *Total Global Strategy: Managing for Worldwide Competitive Advantage,* Prentice Hall, 1992, Chapters 1 and 2.

3. Jean-Pierre Jeannet, *Managing With a Global Mindset,* Financial Times/Prentice Hall, 2000, Chapters 4 and 5.

4. Jeannet, *Managing With a Global Mindset.*

5. C. A. Bartlett and S. Ghoshal, *Managing Across Borders: The Transnational Solution,* Harvard Business School Press, Boston, 1989.

6. Yip, *Total Global Strategy: Managing for Worldwide Competitive Advantage,* Chapter 4, p. 85.

7. From lectures at Templeton College, Oxford University, U.K., by Professor Kunal Basu, Spring 2001, with permission.

8. G. Hamel and C. K. Prahalad, "Do You Really Have A Global Strategy?" *Harvard Business Review,* July–Aug 1985, pp. 139–148.

Strategy Implementation and Control

INTRODUCTION

Crafting a strategy, no matter how complex a task, is substantially easier than successfully implementing one. Strategy formulation is primarily an intellectual and creative act involving analysis and synthesis. Implementation is a hands-on, operations- and action-oriented activity that calls for leadership and managerial skills. Implementing a newly crafted strategy often entails a change in corporate direction and therefore frequently requires a focus on effecting strategic change.

In this final chapter we identify key issues associated with implementing and controlling a chosen strategic direction. We begin by noting that implementation is a top-management responsibility and define it in terms of two principal sets of activities: closing strategic capability gaps and making sure a company maintains strategic focus. Next, we consider how strategy formulation and implementation are linked through learning. With this background, we present an overall conceptual framework that relates a company's strategy to its ultimate performance. This descriptive model has three primary components; the first links strategy, leadership, and corporate purpose; the second describes the organization in terms of its structure, systems, processes, people, and culture, while the third component relates performance to control.

IMPLEMENTATION: RESPONSIBILITY, TASKS, AND LEARNING

Implementation: A Top-Management Responsibility

In today's complex business environment, no single individual—or even the top two or three people—can do all that is required to make a company successful. Success depends on the willingness and ability of all managers to meet not just their own functional or divisional responsibilities but to think about how their actions influence the performance of the company as a whole. Only senior executives can guide this process by rising above detailed action plans, analyzing emerging patterns, and identifying points of maximum leverage for action.[1]

There are three main reasons why top managers must be active participants in the implementation process and not leave this task to others: (1) Only senior executives can resolve the political conflicts that a change in strategic direction inevitably creates by removing the managerial obstacles that can impede successful strategy implementation. (2) Senior managers have the authority to solve problems; teams or middle-level managers are rarely empowered to make the critical decisions to force strategic change. (3) Only senior executives can create the required connections between a company's strategy and capabilities by linking processes, systems, and incentives to intended outcomes.

Converting strategy into action entails numerous activities from acquiring and allocating resources to building capabilities to shaping corporate culture to installing appropriate support systems. These activities can be organized into two broad classes: (1) those directed at *closing strategic capability gaps* and (2) those required for *maintaining strategic focus*.

Closing Strategic Capability Gaps

Strategic capability gaps are substantive disparities in competences, skills, and resources between what customers currently demand or will demand tomorrow and what the organization can deliver. This strategic alignment dimension, therefore, focuses on closing the gap between *what it takes* to succeed in the marketplace and *what the company currently can do*. Examples of activities in this category are developing better technologies, creating faster delivery mechanisms, adopting a stronger branding, and building a stronger distribution network.

Maintaining Strategic Focus

A second set of alignment activities is concerned with maintaining strategic focus. Strategy formulation and implementation are human activities and subject to error, obstruction, or even abuse. To successfully execute a chosen strategy an organization, therefore, must find ways to ensure that *what is said*—by groups and individuals at all levels of the organization—*is in fact done*. Making sure strategic objectives are effectively communicated, allocating the necessary resources, and creating proper incentives for effective alignment are examples of activities in this category.

Linking Strategy Formulation and Implementation Through Learning

Learning is an essential element of strategy development. Implementation is one of the primary ways by which we learn how effective a given strategy is. As soon as we begin to move in a chosen direction, we start to learn (1) about how well attuned the chosen direction is to the competitive environment, (2) about how rivals are likely to respond, and (3) about how well prepared the organization is to carry out its mission.

Though continuous, opportunities for learning are defined in part by the kind of strategy formulation process an organization chooses to adopt. Most companies employ some form of strategic planning. The impetus for imposing structure to the process comes from two main pressures: (1) the need to cope with an increasingly complex range of issues—economic, political, social, and legal on a global scale and (2) the increasing speed with which the competitive environment is changing. A formal system ensures that the required amount of time and resources are allocated to the process, that priorities are set, that activities are integrated and coordinated, and that the right feedback is obtained.

This planning process is usually organized in terms of a *planning cycle*. This cycle often begins with a review at the corporate level of the overall competitive environment and of the corporate guidelines to the various divisions and businesses. Next, divisions and business units are asked to update their long-term strategies and indicate how these strategies fit with the company's major priorities and goals. Third, divisional and business unit plans are reviewed, evaluated, adjusted, coordinated, and integrated in meetings between corporate and divisional/business unit managers. Finally, detailed operating plans are developed at the divisional/business unit level and final approvals are obtained from corporate headquarters.

A formal strategic planning system or planning cycle, by definition, attempts to structure strategy development and implementation as a primarily linear, sequential process. Environmental and competitive changes do not respect a calendar-driven process, however. When a significant new competitive opportunity or challenge emerges, a company cannot afford to wait to respond. This does not mean that formal processes should be abandoned altogether. Rather, it underscores that even though strategy is about crafting a long-term *vision* for an organization, executives should maintain a degree of flexibility about how to get there and preserve options for adapting to change. Strategy formulation and implementation therefore are *not* always sequential activities.

Strategy formulation and implementation at the corporate, business unit, and functional levels can interact in complex ways. A (global strategy) decision to enter a new country, for example, may require strategic change at all three levels—an acquisition or alliance may have to be considered at the corporate level, the company's business model may have to be revisited, and functional processes and support systems may have to be adapted.

Managing Expectations

A good strategy sets out a direction for the future and identifies major challenges. It also frames and manages expectations. Strategic redirection takes time and effort, and results will not always be visible immediately. The time and effort needed to successfully implement a new strategic thrust depend on the magnitude of the change as well as the degree to which the current strategy is entrenched. Figure 9-1 shows a typical change path for a company that has perfected the execution of a strategy that is no longer viable. Inevitably, at first, execution of a new strategy will be less than perfect, reflecting initial confusion about the new direction—both within and outside

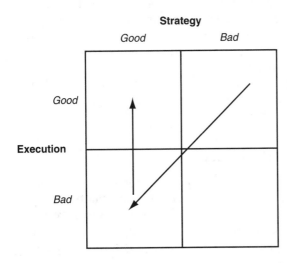

FIGURE 9-1 Managing Expectations for Strategic Change

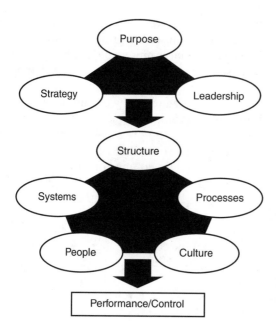

FIGURE 9-2 Strategy and Performance: A Conceptual Framework

the company—and relearning that needs to take place before the new strategy effectively takes hold. Putting a time frame on this adaptation process helps all stakeholders understand the nature of the challenge, sets expectations—for management, employees, suppliers, partners, customers, and the financial markets—and can prevent panic-driven corrections to a sound strategic choice.

STRATEGY AND PERFORMANCE: A CONCEPTUAL FRAMEWORK

Effective implementation is ultimately about obtaining results. Figure 9-2 depicts a conceptual framework that identifies key organizational variables and interactions that define the complex relationship between strategy and a company's ultimate performance. It has three interrelated components. The first links corporate purpose to strategy and leadership. The second describes the organization in terms of five interacting components: structure, systems, processes, people, and culture. The third links a company's definition of performance with two distinct philosophies of exercising control. This framework is helpful in identifying actual or potential challenges and obstacles to successfully implementing a chosen strategic direction. It can also be used to analyze the process of strategic change.

PURPOSE, STRATEGY, AND LEADERSHIP

Increased competitive intensity has created a *greater need* for leadership at all levels of the organization. The higher pace of change and greater uncertainty in the strategic environment also have increased the *difficulty* of providing effective leadership. To prosper in today's competitive environment, keeping up with or adapting to the latest changes is not good enough any more so leaders are actively seeking to regain a measure of control over their destiny by making continuous strategic alignment an organizational core competency itself. In the process, well-known frameworks such as the strategy-structure-systems paradigm are increasingly losing ground to the idea that the effectiveness of strategy implementation is primarily determined by the fit between an organization's purpose, the chosen strategic direction, and the quality of the organization's leadership.

The Strategy-Structure-Systems Paradigm

The so-called strategy-structure-systems paradigm dominated thinking about the role of corporate leaders for many years. Developed in the 1920s, when companies such as General Motors began to experiment with diversification strategies, it held that the key to successfully executing a complex strategy was to create the right organizational structure and disciplined planning and control support systems. Doing so, it was thought, would systematize behavior and minimize ineffective and countereffective actions, and help managers cope with the increased complexity associated with a multibusiness enterprise.

The strategy-structure-systems doctrine remained dominant for most of the twentieth century. It helped companies cope with high growth, integrate their operations horizontally, manage their diversified business portfolios, and expand internationally. The advent of global competition and the technology revolution greatly reduced the doctrine's effectiveness, however. What had been its principal strength—minimizing human initiative— became its major weakness; the new competitive realities called for a different managerial thrust that was focused on developing corporate competencies such as innovation, entrepreneurship, horizontal coordination, and decentralized decision-making.[2]

The New Leadership Focus: From Strategy to Corporate Purpose

Stronger, global competition caused executives to change their focus. Rather than spend time on formulating detailed strategic plans, corporate leaders began to emphasize a broader, long-term strategic intent rooted in a clear sense of corporate purpose. In the face of increasing complexity, they redefined their task from chief strategist to chief facilitator, and sought ways to involve employees at all levels in the strategic management process. Top-executive agendas started to include such items as creating organizational momentum, instilling core values, developing human capital, and recognizing individual accomplishment. In the process, the preoccupation with structural solutions was replaced by a focus on process, and the rationale behind systems was redirected toward supporting the development of capabilities and unleashing human potential rather than guiding employee behavior.[3] The adoption of a broader, more humanistic view of strategic leadership recognizes that strategic discipline and control are secured through commitment, not compliance.

The changes at General Electric over the past decades illustrate this evolution in managerial philosophy. GE once exemplified the strategy-structure-systems philosophy. Its leaders viewed the company primarily as an economic entity and its structure as an aggregation of tasks and responsibilities, while its systems viewed employees as controllable costs. In sharp contrast, GE's current leadership talks about the role of the company as a social institution. The company has adopted a process-based approach to organizational issues focused on clarifying roles and relationships, and it now regards people as organizational assets and embodiers of knowledge.

The top box in Figure 9-2 summarizes these important relationships among a company's strategy, leadership, and sense of purpose. Successful implementation requires that these elements mutually reinforce each other as a basis for obtaining commitment, focus, and control at all levels of the organization.

STRUCTURE, SYSTEMS, PROCESSES, PEOPLE, AND CULTURE

Strategy implementation requires a focus on organizational change. A host of factors—from structural and cultural rigidities to a lack of adequate resources to an adherence to dysfunctional processes—can reduce a company's capacity for absorbing change. It is important, therefore, for executives charged with implementing new strategic directions to understand the dynamics of the various organizational forces at work.

The middle box of Figure 9-2 shows five organizational variables—structure, systems, processes, people, and culture—that are key to creating meaningful organizational change. As shown, it is not clear which of these variables is most important, the driving force for change, or the biggest obstacle to change. What is more, they are interconnected—change in one often requires change in another. Thus, successful implementation of a new strategy often requires change in all variables. As a consequence, strategy implementation efforts that are focused on just one or a few of these variables are doomed to fail. An emphasis on structural solutions—for example, "Let's reorganize"—without paying attention to the other variables is likely to be counterproductive. Style, skills, and superordinate goals—values around which a business is built—can be at least as important as strategy and structure in bringing about fundamental change in an organization. A good strategy alone is not enough.

Structure

To become more competitive, many companies have shed layers of management and adopted flatter organizational structures. The problem of how to organize has evolved from one of dividing up tasks to one focused on issues of coordination. The issue of *structure,* therefore, is not just one of deciding whether to centralize or decentralize decision-making. Rather, it involves identifying dimensions that are crucial to an organization's ability to adapt and evolve strategically, and adopting a structure that allows it to refocus as and when necessary.

In considering structural options, it is important to realize that there is no one right form of organization; each structural solution has specific advantages and drawbacks. What is more, organizations are not homogeneous entities; what is right for one part of an organization or set of tasks might not be the preferred solution for another. No matter what form of organization is used, however, *transparency* is critical; effective strategy implementation cannot occur if lines of authority are blurred or responsibility is ill defined.

Approaches to Organization

Although the strategy-structure-systems paradigm no longer guides management philosophy, strategy and structure are still inextricably linked. Corporate structures typically reflect one of five dominant approaches to organization: (1) *Functional* organizational structures make sense when a particular task requires the efforts of a substantial number of specialists. (2) *Geographically* based structures are useful when a company operates in a diverse set of geographical regions. (3) *Decentralized* (divisional) structures have been found to reduce complexity in a multibusiness environment. (4) *Strategic business units* (SBUs) help define groupings of businesses that share key strategic elements. (5) *Matrix structures* allow multiple channels of authority and are favored when coordination among different interests is key.

The growing importance of human and intellectual capital as a source of competitive advantage has encouraged companies to experiment with new organizational forms. Some are creating organizational structures centered on knowledge creation and dissemination. Others, in a drive to become leaner and more agile, are restricting ownership or control to only those intellectual and physical assets that are critical to their value-creation process. In doing so, they are becoming increasingly virtual and more dependent on an external network of suppliers, manufacturers, and distributors.

Systems and Processes

Having the right *systems* and *processes* enhances organizational effectiveness and facilitates coping with change. Misaligned systems and processes can be a powerful drag on an organization's ability to adapt. Checking what effect, if any, current systems and processes are likely to have on a company's ability to implement a particular strategy is therefore well advised.

Support *systems* such as a company's planning, budgeting, accounting, information, and reward and incentive systems can be critical to successful strategy implementation. While they do not by themselves define a sustainable competitive advantage, superior support systems help a company adapt more quickly and effectively to changing requirements. A well-designed *planning* system ensures that planning is an orderly process, gets the right amount of attention by the right executives, and has a balanced external and internal focus. *Budgeting and accounting* systems are valuable in providing accurate historical data, setting benchmarks and targets, and defining measures of performance. A state-of-the-art *information* system supports all other corporate systems, and it facilitates analysis as well as internal and external communication. Finally, a properly designed *reward and incentive* system is key to creating energy through motivation and commitment.

A *process* is a systematic way of doing things. Processes can be formal or informal; they define organizational roles and relationships and they can facilitate or obstruct change. Some processes look beyond immediate issues of implementation to an explicit focus on developing a stronger capacity for adapting to change. We briefly discuss two of them in greater detail: (1) processes aimed at creating a learning organization and (2) those aimed at fostering continuous improvement.

Creating a Learning Organization

A learning organization is an organization in which everyone—from the lowest-ranking employee on the shop floor to the most senior executive—is involved in identifying and solving problems, enabling it to continuously experiment, change, and improve, thus increasing its capacity to grow, learn, and achieve its purpose.[4] The concept does not imply a specific structure. Rather, it is a vision of and an attitude about what an organization can become.

Senge identifies five disciplines managers should concentrate on in developing a learning organization: (1) encouraging more *systems thinking*—letting employees know how the company really works and how and where they fit in, (2) fostering a *shared vision*—developing a common purpose and commitment, (3) *challenging existing mental models*—questioning old ways of doing things and encouraging outside-the-box thinking, (4) enhancing *team learning*—emphasizing collective over individual contributions and learning, and (5) motivating employees to improve their *personal mastery* of their job.[5] There can be little question that the pursuit of these objectives will help companies adapt more effectively to a changing competitive environment and improve the chances of successfully implementing strategic change.

Fostering Continuous Improvement

Continuous improvement has become critical to maintaining and enhancing competitive advantage. We briefly discuss three approaches: (1) benchmarking, (2) total quality management (TQM), and (3) workouts.

Benchmarking is a useful first step toward establishing a continuous improvement process. It is a multistep technique focused on a comparative evaluation of a process, product, service, or strategy. Initially an internal exercise that companies undertook to improve their efficiency, it was later extended to the identification of *best practices* within or even outside a company's industry. The rigor of the process varies, as does the level of detail involved; Motorola has a five-step process, Xerox's involves twelve. Benchmarking is useful as a learning tool. By learning what competitors or best-in-class companies do better, and how they do it, it offers the potential to (1) enhance competitiveness through continuous improvement of products and processes; (2) foster positive attitudes toward teamwork, cooperation, self-examination, and accepting new and different ideas; and (3) identify ways to redirect a company's strategy for greater effectiveness.

Total quality management (TQM) is a set of management processes and systems developed in the 1950s by quality advocates such as W. Edwards Deming, Joseph Juran, Philip Crosby, and Armand Feigenbaum. It is focused on product and process quality as key drivers behind creating a competitive advantage. TQM relies on five fundamental premises: (1) total commitment, (2) focus on customers, (3) focus on processes, (4) making decisions based on facts, and (5) continuous improvement.[6] It extends to suppliers and other partners in the value-creation process, and relies heavily on the use of statistical quality control methods. For example, FedEx uses service quality indicators to measure and improve quality from the customer's point of view. It uses quality action teams (QATs) to identify problems, establish root causes, and implement solutions. Within two years of initiating its total quality management program, FedEx set company records in two key measurements on the same day: highest daily service level (99.7%) and lowest cost per package.

GE's *workout* initiatives of the 1980s have also received a lot of attention. Designed to eliminate unnecessary bureaucracy, they provided a forum in which employees and executives could work out new ways of responding to competitive challenges. With outside consultants playing a facilitating role, groups of 40 to 100 employees in each of GE's businesses met for several days to share views about what improvements could be made and how. The rules of the process required managers to make on-the-spot decisions on proposed changes, or charter a team to evaluate a proposal by an agreed-upon date. Almost half of GE's work force participated, and considerable productivity increases were realized. The most important benefits probably were not of an operational nature, however. The meetings encouraged front-line employees to challenge the status quo and take the initiative in proposing new ways of doing things. In the process, the workout initiatives helped redefine GE's corporate culture in terms of values such as speed, simplicity, and self-confidence. Quick decision-making modeled speed, the focus on eliminating bureaucracy reinforced simplicity, and the protected decision-making environment and process created self-confidence.[7]

People

Attracting, motivating, and retaining the right *people* have become important strategic issues. After several episodes of mindless downsizing and rightsizing, many companies have recognized how expensive it is to replace knowledge and talent. As a result, much greater emphasis is being placed on attracting, rewarding, and retaining talent at all levels of the organization. A focus on continuous improvement through skill development is an important element of this strategy. Many companies have come to realize that developing tomorrow's skills—individually and collectively—is key to strategic flexibility. Leadership skills, in particular, are in increasing demand. Increased competitive intensity has created a greater need for leadership at all levels of the organization. The higher pace of change and greater uncertainty in the strategic environment also have increased the difficulty of providing effective leadership.[8]

A global study by the Center of Organizational Effectiveness at the University of Southern California, in conjunction with Korn/Ferry International, outlines a ten-step approach to creating an effective talent strategy:

1. Create clear and compelling strategy and vision for the company.
2. Identify the core capabilities needed to excel at this strategy and to continuously improve performance—distinguishing between those skills available externally and those that must be developed in-house.
3. Seek out the best sources of these skills wherever they are available globally—and offer these individuals opportunities to advance and contribute, regardless of nationality.
4. Understand the factors that are most important in attracting and retaining individuals with these key capabilities and in gaining their commitment to the enterprise.
5. Recognize that different groups of employees want different things from work, and that their priorities are likely to shift as they progress through the various stages of their lives and careers.
6. Create multiple career paths (e.g., technical ladders, rotational assignments, and opportunities to join new internal ventures) to replace the declining number of managerial promotion slots in today's flatter organizations.
7. Craft individual development opportunities so employees can build the capabilities that create maximum value for themselves and the company.
8. Hold both employees and management accountable for meeting development objectives and sharing the knowledge they gain with the organization.

9. Tie rewards and recognition to organizational and team performance and enhancement of skills, rather than placing too strong an emphasis on pay-for-individual performance.
10. Seek opportunities to rapidly enhance the company's talent through strategic acquisitions, recognizing that these acquisitions need to be managed differently than traditional mergers.[9]

Culture

A company's *culture*—its guiding philosophies, values, and aspirations—is now recognized as more than a set of fundamental ideas around which the enterprise is built. It defines the core values top executives want to promote throughout the organization, and is key to harnessing and coordinating organizational energies toward specific strategic goals.

Cultural issues tend to get short thrift when a company's ability to effect or absorb change is analyzed. Yet, soft issues such as the basic personality of the top management group—What attitude does the group project to the rest of the organization? How does it spend its time? What efforts get rewarded and rebuked?—are extremely important when it comes to successfully implementing a change in strategic direction. Symbolism is equally important. Companies tend to attract people, fund projects, and publicize accomplishments in areas where they are most successful. Strategies designed to alter this focus should recognize this fact.

As knowledge becomes more important to global competitiveness, three cultural change themes are heard with greater frequency: (1) encouraging "boundaryless" behavior, (2) creating a culture of innovation and entrepreneurship, and (3) competing on the basis of speed.

Encouraging Boundaryless Behavior

Cross-functional decision-making, based on the elimination of artificial barriers imposed by organizational structure, functional domains, or formal processes and procedures, will be increasingly critical to successful strategy implementation. One approach to creating such a culture of *boundaryless* behavior focuses on organizing around tasks and missions. When a new product needs to be launched, or best practices need to be instilled throughout the company, an ad-hoc task force can cut through traditional bureaucracies and hierarchical structures more freely than can individual executives. Cross-company training, networking, and a focus on more-horizontal communication across organizational units also are helpful in this respect.

Developing a Culture of Innovation and Entrepreneurship

Balancing strategic focus and discipline with a capacity to be creative and think outside the box is a challenge for many companies. Just as individuals differ in their creative abilities, so do organizations differ in their abilities to translate the talents of employees into concrete new ideas and action. Creating a sustainable capacity for innovation and entrepreneurship—an ability to consistently develop and launch successful new and improved products and services, improve products, and enter new markets—requires careful analysis of existing processes, procedures, and dominant cultures. Keeping business units relatively small, partnering with other organizations, and designating parts of the organization a "skunk works" are useful. However, as experience at companies such as 3M has shown, embedding an entrepreneurial spirit requires top-management commitment to and institutionalization of innovation-friendly processes, procedures, and reward and incentive systems. This means, among other things, setting explicit targets for innovation, motivating employees and giving them the time and resources to pursue new ideas, accepting occasional failures as necessary learning on the path to long-run success, taking calculated risks, backing proposals that merit support, and celebrating and rewarding success.

Toward a Culture of Speed

In Chapter 5 we noted that speed has emerged as an increasingly important element of business unit strategy. Fostering a fast culture poses its own unique challenges. Entrepreneurial firms generally have an easier time adjusting to the requirements of speed because they tend to be less bureaucratic and their existing cultures are less entrenched. For most companies, however, developing a speed-conducive culture requires considerable time and investment; calls for fundamental changes in systems, procedures, and processes; and requires learning new skills. Techniques such as business process reengineering can help identify opportunities for accelerating parts of a company's business model. Often, new metrics must be adopted to measure and reinforce the strategic focus on speed, and investments must be made in technology. Most importantly, however, everyone in the firm must adopt a new mind-set that is focused on speed.

PERFORMANCE AND CONTROL

A major premise of this book is that strategic and operational performance should be measured in terms of value creation to customers. Everything else follows. Value to shareholders and other stakeholders accrues when customer needs and expectations are met or exceeded. Companies that better meet customer needs typically are more adept at developing competitive advantages and core competencies. Finally, a true customer orientation helps companies anticipate and leverage market opportunities in times of rapid change.

In Chapter 3 we discussed a number of techniques for measuring and evaluating performance at different levels in the organization from economic value added to gap analysis to the Balanced Scorecard. As noted in Chapter 7, most of these schemes are focused on *outcome control*—the attainment of specific targets in pursuit of specific goals. Outcome control is principally achieved by altering the incentive structure for business units, executive teams, and individual managers. When changing an existing corporate culture is key to enhancing performance or implementing a new strategic direction, outcome management might not be enough, however. A *behavior control* style of management might be called for. Under behavior control, the company directly monitors the behavior of specific business units, executive teams, or individual managers, for example, through the approval of capital expenditure requests or specific hiring or promotion decisions.

Figure 9-3 summarizes the key differences between these two approaches as evidenced by how a company's structure, systems, and procedures are aligned with its chosen strategic direction. In practice, companies practicing outcome control will also ask behavioral control questions and vice versa. The differences between the two philosophies are real, however, and affect how corporate systems and processes are used, and shape a company's culture.

Outcome Control	Behavior Control
• Structure: Independent, self-contained units • Rewards, Incentives: Substantial part of overall compensation, tied to a single, quantifiable objective • Resource Allocation: Tight expenditure controls • People: Focus on industry experience, aligning incentives with performance • Corporate Office: Small, focused on analyzing results	• Rewards, Incentives: Focus on long-term career progression; performance measurement based on multiple quantitative and qualitative goals • People: Internal career paths; active career development focused on industry and company-specific experience • Culture: Focus on common corporate culture designed to allow managers to move freely among divisions • Corporate Office: Experienced corporate managers function as advisors and monitors

FIGURE 9-3   Outcome and Behavior Control: Key Dimensions

A FINAL WORD

As strategy implementation and control are increasingly being defined in terms of strategic alignment, a growing number of corporations are exploring new forms of organization, which emphasize horizontal communication and coordination over traditional, vertical hierarchical decision-making. A *Fortune* article describes today's managerial challenge as the ultimate paradox: (1) keep everything running efficiently and profitably, while, at the same time, (2) change everything.[10]

This new focus on reinventing the corporation reflects a major shift in managerial thinking. Instead of thinking about the strategic environment as essentially in equilibrium, subject to occasional shocks and disturbances that strategies must confront, the new paradigm emphasizes constant, often chaotic change. Trying to control things back into some stable equilibrium is all but impossible in this new world; there is no alternative but to get comfortable with continuous change.

NOTES

1. Thomas M. Hout and John C. Carter, "Getting It Done: New Roles for Senior Executives," *Harvard Business Review,* Nov. 1995, p. 133.
2. Christopher Bartlett and Sumantra Goshal, "Changing The Role Of Top Management: From Strategy To Purpose," *Harvard Business Review,* Nov. 1994, p. 79.
3. It is, of course, no coincidence that during this same period the resource-based view

of strategic thinking overtook the industrial economics perspective. See Chapter 1.
4. Richard L. Daft, *Management,* Fourth edition, The Dryden Press, 1997, p. 751.
5. Peter Senge, *The Fifth Discipline: The Art and Practice of Learning Organizations,* New York: Doubleday/Currency, 1990.
6. B. Bergman and B. Klefsjö, *Quality: From Customer Needs to Customer Satisfaction,* London: McGraw-Hill, 1994.

7. GE's Two-Decade Transformation: Jack
   Welch's Leadership, Harvard Business
   School Case Study 9-399-150, Rev. Jan. 2000.
8. John P. Kotter, *The Leadership Factor,* New
   York: The Free Press, 1988, p. 12.
9. David Feingold and Susan Mohrman,
   What Do Employees Really Want?

The Perception vs. The Reality, Center
for Effective Organizations, University
of Southern California, and Korn/Ferry
International, 2001.
10. John Huey, "Managing in the Midst of
    Chaos," *Fortune,* April 5, 1993, pp. 38–48.

Index

Figures are indicated by the italicized letter *f* followed by the italic page number.